INVISIBLE MONUMENTS

Books by Howard Mansfield

Cosmopolis
In the Memory House
Skylark
The Same Ax, Twice
The Bones of the Earth
Turn & Jump
Dwelling in Possibility
Sheds
Summer Over Autumn
The Habit of Turning the World Upside Down
Chasing Eden
I Will Tell No War Stories

Editor
Where the Mountain Stands Alone

For Children
Hogwood Steps Out

INVISIBLE MONUMENTS

TRIBUTE, MEMORY, AND THE SUMMONING OF THE PAST

HOWARD MANSFIELD

LP
LYONS PRESS
Essex, Connecticut

LYONS PRESS

An imprint of The Globe Pequot Publishing Group, Inc.
64 South Main St.
Essex, CT 06426
www.globepequot.com

British Library Cataloguing in Publication Information available

Library of Congress Cataloging-in-Publication Data available

ISBN 9781493097289 (cloth) | ISBN 9781493097296 (epub)

Once again, and always, for Dr. B. A. Millmoss

In ancient times, the Achilpa carried their sacred pole with them as they traveled in the Australian Outback. The divine Numbakula created the pole from a gum tree, anointed it with blood, and climbed it into sky where he disappeared. With their pole, the Achilpa were at the center of the universe. "Once, when the pole was broken, the entire clan were in consternation; they wandered about aimlessly for a time, and finally lay down on the ground together and waited for death to overtake them."

—MIRCEA ELIADE, *THE SACRED AND THE PROFANE* (1959)

"When marble, sandstone and granite have crumbled to atoms, these monuments will remain untouched by the destroying hand of time."

—E. P. HARRIS, PROFESSOR OF CHEMISTRY,
AMHERST COLLEGE, MASSACHUSETTS,
CATALOGUE OF THE MONUMENTAL BRONZE COMPANY (1882)

CONTENTS

The Monumental Bronze Company created a standing army of zinc Civil War soldiers. A page from the company catalog, October 1882.

INTRODUCTION: BRINGING THE BONES HOME

"The Vietnamese believe a person should be buried twice," says Viet Thanh Nguyen. "The first time, in a field removed from home and village, the earth is allowed to eat the flesh. The second time, the survivors must disinter what remains. They wash the bones with their own hands, and then they bury the bones once more, this time closer to the living."

We do the same. When we commission memorials, we are trying to bring the bones closer to home. The memorials we build are a second burial. In all the current controversies about what to build and how, and what to tear down, we've lost track of why we build monuments. We want the counsel of our ancestors—edited and chiseled into stone.

But most monuments melt into invisibility. We argue about their design, dedicate them with grand ceremonies, and walk away. They are seldom noticed again. Daily life pushes them aside. Tons of the finest granite, marble, and bronze prove to be insubstantial, vaporized by our indifference. We fail to summon our ancestors.

The stones don't talk to us; muteness defines monuments. "What strikes one most about monuments is that one doesn't notice them. There is nothing in this world as invisible as monuments," said the Austrian writer Robert Musil in 1927. And yet we are in the midst of a boom in building monuments. We want to bring the bones home.

Invisible Monuments explores how we try to keep our ancestors near, looking at moments of commemoration or the failure to commemorate. Each chapter explores the invisibility of many monuments and the few that succeed:

- The Cenotaph—the empty tomb—in London is a decidedly humble monument that brought forth a strong emotional response after World War I, becoming the locus of grief. Our era's equivalent is a low, dark wall on the Mall, the Vietnam Veterans Memorial, that has become, as General Colin Powell says, "an altar, a shrine, a temple, a church."
- A celebrated, much-pictured monument that doesn't have the emotional charge and significance that it once held. On the anniversary of the Battle of Bunker Hill, I visited Charlestown to witness the challenge of keeping the American Revolution close to us, of recalling the bloody fight at Bunker Hill, on an ideal summer day for picnics and parades. On such a fine day, the presiding granite obelisk approached invisibility.
- The forced invisibility of the African Burial Grounds in Manhattan and Portsmouth, New Hampshire, which have been rediscovered. These graveyards were destroyed in keeping with America's "mortuary apartheid." An unmarked grave, a buried and defiled grave, is also a telling marker.
- The sad fate of the Irish immigrants building America's railroads in the nineteenth century, many killed on the job to be buried in unmarked graves. Researching another story, I came across what may have been the largest labor riot in the history of northern New England, one that's never been written about. These Irish workers were reviled. They were denied their names in news reports, and in death when they were left behind in the woods of New Hampshire.
- A grieving family's memorial to a son lost in World War II, built stone by stone on the family's farm, which still draws thousands to an outdoor "Cathedral of the Pines."
- A Ferris wheel, stopped forever after a tragic accident, abandoned to rust, which becomes a private monument for a five-year-old boy.
- An unusual monument, one that doesn't look to the past like other monuments. It is a tribute to the future. This is a clock being built

deep in a mountain, a clock that is meant to run for ten thousand years. The clock is a technological sleight of hand, but even more so, it is a virtuoso act of optimism. The conjurers of this clock want us to believe that another ten thousand years of civilization is possible.

- And lastly, a monument hiding on museum walls. The great landscape painters of the nineteenth century, sometimes called the Hudson River School, weren't out just to paint pretty pictures. They were chasing a moment of insight when they would see this new nation clearly. Their paintings taught Americans how to see wilderness and laid the bounds for many of our national parks.

My goal with these stories is similar to that of the landscape painters. I want to refresh our sight so we can look anew at the monuments around us and engage in a call and response with our history.

After the Civil War, towns and cities summoned a standing army of zinc soldiers, ready-made statues that could be ordered from a catalog. One company that sold these statues promised that zinc would "last as long as the Pyramids of Egypt." Few things do. And that doesn't matter. It's the moment of commemoration that matters, the washing of the bones and their reburial.

Anthropologist Michael Blakely, who oversaw the study of Manhattan's African Burial Ground, says, "I sometimes think that we should be called *homo reminiscens*, not sapiens, that what distinguishes us is that we are the memorializers."

We are like the ancient Achilpa in Australia's outback. They carried their sacred pole, the center of their universe. As long as they had their pole, they were sure of their place in the cosmos; their ride around the sun was a ceremonial procession in a greater drama. The mundane was sacred. And when the pole broke, when they lost contact with their ancestors, they lay down and wept.

PART I

"I HAD A SIMPLE IMPULSE TO CUT INTO THE EARTH."

The gun carriage bearing the Unknown Warrior approaches the Cenotaph in London for the unveiling ceremony by King George V on the second anniversary of the armistice ending World War I, November 11, 1920. The Unknown Warrior was interred that day in Westminster Abbey. HORACE NICHOLLS, IMPERIAL WAR MUSEUMS (Q 31513).

THE EMPTY TOMB, THE WALL, AND THE DISAPPEARING MONUMENT

I.

It was meant to be a temporary memorial, erected for a parade: a tribute that says, "Never forget"—just for this day. But from the moment it was there, the mourners came by the thousands, lining up deep into the night, waiting for hours. Young widows, mothers, brothers, fathers. They paused before the memorial, a cenotaph, an empty tomb, and filled it with their grief. Some wept, some kneeled in prayer, some stood looking, as if awaiting an answer. *Fill this void in my heart. Lift this suffocating emptiness.* By the end of the week, more than 1.25 million had joined the silent procession. Britain and its empire had lost 1.1 million soldiers in the Great War. Millions more were wounded. No fallen soldiers, no remains, had come home. The mourners that first day left behind a mountain of flowers ten feet deep. The flowers had to be cleared before a parade that morning.

The Cenotaph was designed quickly, on short notice, by architect Edwin Lutyens. It was built in eleven days out of wood and plaster, painted white, and set out on the route for the Peace Day Parade in London on July 19, 1919, to officially mark the end of World War I. The war had ended in November 1918. The Treaty of Versailles was signed three weeks before the parade. Prime Minister David Lloyd George wanted a monument for soldiers to salute as they walked past.

The design is spare, elegant, a pylon that steps back as it rises over thirty-five feet and is capped by a casket. The word *cenotaph* is derived from the Greek for *empty tomb*—it is a visible tribute to the invisible dead. Lutyens described it as an "empty tomb uplifted on a high pedestal." This is not the usual memorial stone cross, or a great general on his horse. "It is the common sense of the design that has surprised us, used as we are, to anything but common sense in our monuments," said the art critic for *The Times of London*. "It says simply and precisely what it has to say, like a Greek Epitaph; and people find that they prefer this to nymphs and wreaths and crowns and pilasters that say nothing in particular." Its restraint is noble.

The visit to the Cenotaph was a procession, a ritual. People left flowers and wreaths. They made contact with the austere monument. It became the locus of their loss. "The whole point of the Cenotaph," said Lutyens, "is that it should be motionless in the center of the crowd." Mourners inscribed it with their "own thoughts, reveries, sadnesses," said historian Jay Winter. "It says so much because it says so little."

The public, and the press led by *The Times of London*, adopted the temporary monument of wood and plaster. They asked that it stay. The response surprised the cabinet, but within weeks they commissioned a permanent memorial. The Cenotaph was rebuilt in "good Portland Stone," a limestone that gives many of London's buildings their solidity. Portland stone was the formal suit for official London, the stone used in Buckingham Palace, the British Museum, and St. Paul's Cathedral.

Lutyens refined his design. No single line is completely straight. Each has the "subtle curvatures" of entasis, as in the Parthenon. "The difference is almost imperceptible, yet sufficient to give it a sculpturesque quality and a life, that cannot pertain to rectangular blocks of stone," he said. Lutyens made thirty-three pages of calculations, marking his drawings, showing where the four corners were to meet at an imagined point about one thousand feet up, and the horizontal lines in the center of a circle nine hundred feet below ground. The surface is unadorned, except for, on each narrow end, a wreath of laurel in stone and two inscriptions:

The years for the war in Roman numerals and below, "The Glorious Dead." There are rings on each long side to hold flags for ceremonies. The Church of England's bishops lobbied for a cross to be added; Lutyens refused.

The limestone Cenotaph was dedicated by the king the following year, in 1920, and again it was buried in flowers. Mourners waited up to four hours in "slowly moving queues" that were four and six abreast. "Flower-laden" pilgrims, mostly women, wound around the streets and bridges of London to be near "that strangely wonderful memorial," said *The Daily Mirror.* "An amazing scene unparalleled in the history of London." From dawn until midnight, on fair days and in the "pitiless drizzle of rain" and fog, all that could be heard was "the slow shuffle of thousands of feet." "As we pass the Cenotaph, the agony, the sweat, the speechless valour of the dark, fast-fading years all came back with swelling pride and tears," said *The Daily Telegraph.* "The pent-up emotion . . . is quick and sharp."

After the Great War, mourning rituals were hastily invented: The Cenotaph had been designed and built in weeks for the July parade. Months later, on Armistice Day, following King George V's proclamation calling for a moment of "perfect stillness," mourners stood in silence for two minutes. The next year, the permanent Cenotaph was joined by the Tomb of the Unknown Warrior in Westminster Abbey. A flag-draped coffin was borne to Westminster on a horse-drawn gun carriage, pausing at the Cenotaph. Two big Union Jacks covered the monument. Big Ben "boomed out louder, it seemed, than ever one hears it even in the stillness of dawn," said *The Times of London.* The king "released the flags. . . . They fell away. . . . Big Ben ceased; and the very pulse of Time stood still. In silence, broken only by a nearby sob, the great multitude bowed its head." The procession continued to Westminster. The highest commanders of the war were pallbearers; the king scattered soil from France on the coffin. "All this was to stir such memories and emotions as might have made the very stones cry out," said one witness. It seemed ancient—the silence, the empty tomb, and the tomb of the unknown—but this was an invented tradition. In the first week, 1.25 million would visit the Tomb of the Unknown Warrior.

The soldiers marched past the Cenotaph four abreast. If the empire's dead could have marched past, it would have taken three and half days, said the head of the Imperial War Graves Commission. It was really one march, from enlistment to death, an army of the surrogate dead, said Goeff Dyer. "If we followed the line, it would take us back to another photograph, of men marching away to war. These two images are really simply two segments of a single picture of the long march through the war," said Dyer. "There is a single column of men, so long that by the time those at the back are marching off from the recruiting stations, heading to trains, those at the front—the dead—are marching past the Cenotaph."

Half of the British war dead were never found or identified. The rest, it was decided, would be left across the Channel. They were not coming home to be buried. Their bodies belonged forever to the state, to the British Empire. The public protested; they petitioned the king and the prime minister "for the only consolation left us," but the government held firm: Moving the dead would be a "violation . . . of the desire of the dead themselves." Soldiers would be buried in cemeteries on foreign soil, uniform in design, each with an identical stone with the name, regiment, rank, religion, and date of death (no birth date). Families could add an epitaph limited to sixty-six characters, including spaces, subject to strict review, at their own expense. If their boy was among the missing—at war's end 315,000 had not been found in France and Belgium alone—his name would be inscribed on a memorial. At one monument at Thiepval (also designed by Lutyens), a towering series of arches sheltered more than seventy-two thousand names, almost all volunteers killed in the Battle of the Somme in 1916, a crushing loss that "marked the end of an age of vital optimism in British life that has never been restored," said historian John Keegan.

"If you ask where is the Picasso of England or the Ezra Pound of France, there is only one probable answer: Still in the trenches," said the art critic Robert Hughes. British soldiers had a one-in-two chance of being killed, wounded, or taken prisoner. More than 2.25 million were wounded. Two years after the war, sixty-five thousand veterans were receiving disability pensions for "neurasthenia"—shell shock. A generation of men in their twenties was depleted. Most of the men, just starting out in life, had not married. Their mourners were parents, not wives. Still, there were so many young widows that the mourning period was shortened, and the etiquette was updated for formal mourning dress.

Most people had expected a short war. During the hundred years of the "long peace," the fourteen wars fought in Europe had been relatively brief. The boys left in August. They'd be home by Christmas. Some marched off in "pals battalions"—entire soccer clubs or villages off on an adventure together, a "second boyhood." Off they went to industrial-scale slaughter. When they were killed together, it was like a meteor hitting a village, wiping out a generation. The war dragged on for four years.

With empty-casket funerals, no proper last rites, no graves to visit, many families were unmoored, reduced in their grief to being bystanders. In the 1920s and 1930s—the "interwar years"—Britain was obsessed with death, say historians. Families made pilgrimages to old battlefields scarred by miles of trenches on the Western Front. The YMCA and the Salvation Army organized tours. The British public put up about one hundred thousand memorials—crosses, obelisks, and statues by village roadsides, railroad stations, and factories; rolls of honor in schools and churches; stained-glass windows; and many dedicated civic buildings. ("Every English highway is now one continuous memorial avenue," said one guide.) They reached out to their fallen soldiers through mediums; they listened for "rappings" at midnight séances, shared "spirit photos" and "automatic writing," messages from the dead guiding a pen in the hand of the living. Belief in spiritualism was "spreading like wildfire." There were more than three hundred spiritualist churches and popular books in which authors conversed with dead sons. Arthur Conan Doyle, who had lost his brother, and his brother-in-law, and his eldest son, Kingsley, put aside Sherlock Holmes to talk at the Spiritualists' National Union memorial service in Royal Albert Hall. He had been talking with Kingsley. The dead didn't come home, but death did.

The mourners at the Cenotaph had lost everything in the Great War. They'd lost the Old Europe. The old order lay on the other side of the "war to end all wars," and there was no way back. The First World War was, as historian Barbara Tuchman said, a "path burnt across history."

To be with millions united in mourning is a comfort, but still what we're witnessing is a procession of loss that is private, an absence that will have to be lived out over breakfast-lunch-and-dinner, over Christmases and homecomings, graduations and weddings. Each person passing the Cenotaph had lost a brother, son, husband, father, uncle, grandfather. When you step back from the big statistics and come down to a widow at tea, alone, the loss is staggering.

Any monument that we stand before asks something of us. Think of monuments as the first part of a call and response, as in music, as in worship. We bring our sense of history to the present, otherwise the granite/marble/limestone/bronze before us will be mute. The Cenotaph was a powerful synthesis of memorial and mourner, of call and response. During the war, grand plans had been floated for a "Great War Memorial" triumphal arch and a massive "Hall of Memory" with a domed rotunda to rival St. Paul's Cathedral, but the British public chose a modest, plain tribute. Millions, in their grief, chose the Cenotaph to be Britain's national war monument.

II.

The Vietnam Veterans Memorial in Washington may be our era's Cenotaph. When I am facing the wall of names, I feel it my gut. It's visceral. These two monuments are a home for grief.

At the Vietnam Veterans Memorial, you don't just stand and look; you walk slowly down into the earth. At the center, the apex, as architect Maya Lin calls it, where the two walls meet like an opened book, you are six feet under. To the left is the Lincoln Memorial, to the right is the Washington Monument, and before you are 58,276 names of young men. Most of them never made it beyond their twenty-first birthdays. Your visit is a procession, "a passage to an awareness about loss," Lin says. She has slowed you down and made you pay attention. There's no turning away from the names. Maya Lin makes the earth here vibrate just a little bit.

"How could this gravestone to those who died in America's most controversial and most unpopular war come to occupy such a wonderful, remarkable place in America's collective heart?" General Colin Powell asked at the twenty-fifth anniversary of the wall in 2007. "How could it have become an altar, a shrine, a temple, a church?"

Maya Lin was a twenty-one-year-old Yale undergraduate when her design was chosen over fourteen hundred other entries in a national competition. About a week before the deadline for the competition, she was in Professor Vincent Scully's history of architecture class. The famous professor was showing slides of Lutyens's Memorial to the Missing of the Somme at Thiepval, with its seventy-two thousand names. The design competition required a horizontal Vietnam memorial listing all the names of the American soldiers who had been killed. Her design was set, but she was struggling with the text she had to submit to explain her plan. She saw the pictures of Thiepval and began "writing furiously." "You go through the gaping mouth of the monument, the names are surrounding you, and you're left looking out on a quiet field, crosses and headstones, but you can't go beyond," she says. Lutyens's design had no steps from the monument into the cemetery. "There's a separation." The living and the dead part ways.

Lin had seen the power of enshrined names up close. She was moved by Yale's memorial rotunda. "I have never been able to resist touching the names cut into these marble walls, and no matter how busy or crowded the place is, a sense of quiet, a reverence, surrounds those names. Throughout my freshman and sophomore years, the stonecutters were carving in by hand the names of those killed in the Vietnam War, and I think it left a lasting impression on me."

Before she began her design, she visited the site set aside for the memorial on the National Mall. While others may have focused on their design in isolation, she wanted her work to be a part of the earth.

Lin had grown up in Ohio exploring ancient earthworks, including the prehistoric Serpent Mound, the mysterious "effigy mound," a snake uncoiling for almost a quarter mile. On the summer solstice, the snake's head aligns with the setting sun. The snake—a symbol whose meaning we can only guess—a mediator between worlds? guardian of rebirth and transformation?—was a powerful creature commanding a high ridge. The Ohio earthworks were another source of her inspiration.

When she designs, she follows her intuition. Standing at the memorial site, she knew what she would do. "I had a simple impulse to cut into the earth," she said. "I imagined taking a knife and cutting into the earth, an initial violence and pain that in time would heal." She wanted the memorial to be an "interface, between our world and the quieter, darker, more peaceful world beyond."

Lin was forthright about death. "I sought a design that would bring the viewer to an honest acceptance of the deaths of those individuals," she says. "As opposed to pretending it never happened, you have to look it straight in the eye. Then you can turn around and walk back out into the light." If you want to talk about valor, patriotism, or realpolitik—that's your choice, and it's all in play—but first face the wall, face death. Stand and grieve. We don't do that enough, she says.

The Vietnam Veterans Memorial is honest—it says, "Here is death." It's modest. It creates a place to think, she says, but it doesn't tell us what to think. It's intimate. The lettering is small—smaller than that used on most memorials. Reading the names is a private act in a public space.

"Anyone can relate to a name," says Laura Palmer, who showed up in Saigon right out of college to cover the war. "If you've given birth to a child, if you've held a baby in your arms, baptized someone and say, 'I name you,' this wall will break your heart."

Once Lin won, she had to fight hard to protect her design. All her details are precise. Review boards and the architects hired to execute the design wanted changes. They wanted the names listed alphabetically so it would be "easier to use," so visitors wouldn't have to first look up a name in a directory. She showed them how more than six hundred Smiths would pile up—how would that make people feel? She asked them, "You don't think people will take the time, a little time" to look up the names? The names are listed chronologically, as each soldier died, with the first and last deaths meeting at the center, making a continuous circle. The names run into the earth and emerge from the earth.

They wanted to add text and did succeed in adding a few words that nobody notices. They wanted the names larger. It was "unheard of" to use the small type size she specified. But that small type drew people closer; it wasn't monumental. They wanted to use a lighter-colored stone, and they wanted to use a thicker cut. But she held firm: the wall would have a thin face of polished black granite. "The wall dematerializes," she says. It's a "pure and reflective surface that would allow visitors the chance to see themselves with the names." It's the thin face of a cut into the earth. She sees it as a geode, a rock split and polished, like the one her brother had when they were children.

The memorial came to be called the Healing Wall, but not for everyone. The power of the Vietnam Veterans Memorial is what it allows us to forget, says novelist and professor Viet Thanh Nguyen. "It remembers certain people and excludes many others," says Nguyen, who was born in Vietnam during the "American War." About two million Vietnamese were killed. If their names were on the wall, it would stretch across the Mall and continue for two miles. As he sees it, this is a "healing wall" without a true reckoning. "Wars are fought twice," Nguyen says. "The first time on the battlefield, the second time in memory."

Other critics saw dishonor and shame. They wanted the antheses of her design: a shining white marble wall, raised up, with statues, flags, patriotic inscriptions. They wanted the memorial equivalent of a brass band and a banner proclaiming, "Mission accomplished." They refused to confront the death of these fifty-eight thousand young men. They refused to grieve. They knew nothing about the power of the Cenotaph or Thiepval. At those memorials the pull of absence is a vortex.

When we visit the wall, we enter the story. The noise of Washington falls away as we walk downhill. Talk stops. It's as if we are "entering a force field," says one visitor. "The Mall largely disappears from view, and the memorial draws you into its embrace," says another. When it rains, say many visitors, it looks like the wall is weeping.

In his poem "Facing It," Yusef Komunyakaa describes his visit:

My black face fades,
hiding inside the black granite.
I said I wouldn't
dammit: No tears.
I'm stone. I'm flesh.
My clouded reflection eyes me
like a bird of prey, the profile of night
slanted against morning. I turn
this way—the stone lets me go.
I turn that way—I'm inside
the Vietnam Veterans Memorial
again, depending on the light
to make a difference.

At the memorial when you touch the names, says noted writer Louis Menand, "you are also touching the shadow of your hand, coming out of the darkness."

From the first, visitors began leaving things at the wall—letters, flowers, medals, army boots, ponchos, teddy bears, wedding photos, small models they had made, a pro-war book that had been shot up. These items are powerful. They're gifts, tributes, flares of grief shot into the sky, a farewell, a regret, a protest, a wail of *why?*, a bid to break the mute distance between the living and the dead. No one expected that visitors would leave these offerings.

Every day all the objects are gathered and taken to a National Park Service warehouse, where they are cataloged. Daily, another monument grows. This is what we do to keep the dead near. We bring them dog tags, Zippo lighters, Bibles, and letters written on stationery from the hotels nearby—one last letter, one last goodbye. *I meant to say . . . I'm sorry I never said . . . We were so young . . . You're still 24. I'm 71 . . . I miss you. I love you.*

The Vietnam Veterans Memorial changed how we mourn, says historian Kristin Hass. Psychiatrists write to thank Maya Lin. Under their care, a veteran's last step in recovery is to visit the wall. It helps them.

"The important thing to know about the Vietnam Veterans Memorial is that it made memorials matter again," says Hass. And it led to a boom in building new monuments. Before the wall, no war memorial had been built in Washington since 1936. (The big Marine Corps War Memorial, the Iwo Jima statue, was dedicated in 1954 near Arlington National Cemetery.) Other monuments now crowd Washington: World War I, World War II, Dwight D. Eisenhower, Korean War, Navy, Air Force, National Guard, Black Civil War Veterans, Disabled Veterans, Native American Veterans, Vietnam Women's Memorial. And in the works, there is a Global War on Terrorism Memorial and one for Desert Shield and Desert Storm. The Mall has become a "war theme park," says historian Marilyn Young. They're trying to bury the wall and not let it have the last word, she says. "You have to keep building things on top of it to say no to it."

In the nation's capital, memory is assembled, contested, revised. It's shaped by fashion and constituent groups competing to memorialize their view of the past, competing to say who's remembered and in what manner. (If democracy is an experiment, so is our commemoration of the wars fought to defend it.) As Viet Thanh Nguyen said, wars are fought twice: first in battle and then in memory. The winner gets to write the moral to the tale in stone.

Many of the recent monuments, in Washington and elsewhere, are wan assemblages of walls of names and chunks of fragmented geometry. They're static. There's a fountain, a statue, a flag, a wall or two. They are not sites of pilgrimage. After the dedication ceremonies, they too often melt to invisibility. Tourists may soak their hot feet in the fountains, as they do in the World War II Memorial's wading pool; skateboarders may be tempted by the ramps and railings, or may be the only visitors, as they are at the broad marble expanse of the Freedom Plaza (a failed 1980 installation on Pennsylvania Avenue).

The Cenotaph was regally silent, and it spoke to millions. The Vietnam Veterans Memorial speaks to us. But most monuments are mute. We face them in a kind of standoff and move on. We read the plaque, take in a blur of names as if they were the raised dots of Braille, fiddle with our phones, dismiss the scene with a glance, and leave. They are, says historian Jay Winter, "simply white noise in stone."

At war memorials, the questions are, How close do we want the dead? How directly can we look at loss and suffering? Do we submerge their deaths in stories of valor and sacrifice, national unity and patriotism, or military preparedness? Do we use those stories to shield us from death?

At the Florence American Cemetery and Memorial in Italy, covering seventy acres, an inscription implores visitors to "not mourn with the parents of the dead who are with us. Rather comfort them. Let their burden be lightened by the glory of the dead. . . . It is by honor that the end of life is cheered." At the Normandy American Cemetery in France, the dead are presided over by a statue of a muscular Nureyev-like dancer leaping heavenward, a balletic, Olympic stretch above tragedy: "Spirit of American Youth Rising from the Waves." It's all very grand, like something you'd see at the entrance to a world's fair or some official Euro-governing headquarters.

It's not that courage and patriotism aren't animating ideas—they hold countries together—but at memorials they can camouflage the fact that war is about killing, giving us an easy exit from the truth. When the Marine Corps Memorial was dedicated, President Eisenhower left the ceremony early, angry some say, at the failure to acknowledge the cost in lives to take the island of Iwo Jima. (One-third of all Marines killed in World War II died on that island. Three of the six men in the famous flag-raising photo were killed.)

At the Cenotaph and the Vietnam Veterans Memorial, grief is front and center. The dead are exposed to view. At each place, the public completed the memorial, they created a ritual, they lined up late into the night to leave flowers; they stood still, having found the name they came to see, to touch, and maybe to trace, and then they left the young man, gone more than sixty years, a handwritten letter.

Colin Powell was right: The wall is "an altar, a shrine, a temple, a church." It's a threshold, a place where we cross over from the mundane toward the unknowable. It's an axis mundi, where we can stand in the center of our grief, and it's a Serpent Mound—it is earth and more than earth—something that points us to a deeper truth.

What will the wall mean in forty years? No telling. The call and response—the emotion and memories—will have changed.

III.

Since Maya Lin's wall "made memorials matter again," we have been debating the importance of memorials—Are we building too many? What makes a proper memorial? Lin's success revived an old debate. We have been saying goodbye to a certain kind of monument—the heroic punctuation to an era, the monument that is a landmark in the historic narrative we all share. Those monuments were story bearers that didn't need decoding. This language was so common that after the Civil War, a city or a small town could order its own Civil War soldier, cast in zinc, and set him out in the city park or on the common, with the appropriate, lengthy speeches and benedictions, everyone dressed in their Sunday best. The Monumental Bronze Company of Bridgeport, Connecticut, made thousands of soldiers—supplying many of the twenty-five hundred zinc soldiers for the North and five hundred for the South, a ready-made assembly line of memory (the metal conveniently bluish-gray). Even as the North and South told different stories, there was no question about what a Civil War memorial should look like.

But there was already what could be called commemoration fatigue. Just a year after the Civil War, William Dean Howells, a leading literary figure and the editor of *The Atlantic*, worried that Americans in a rush to remember the war might raise a "much greater standing-army in bronze and marble than would have been needed for the suppression of any future rebellion." The country, said other critics, was plagued by a legion of dreary zinc soldiers, a standing army of cliché. Another staple of American cities, the equestrian statue, also came to be scorned. After a dozen of these were posted to Washington's streets in a span from 1853 to 1909, architects and city planners wanted to clear public spaces of equestrian statues. ("New Statues for District Shun Horse," said a *Washington Post* headline in 1926.) As the horse was vanquished by the electric streetcar and the automobile, so, too, did it lose its place of honor.

But once we have banished the pedestal and statue, the obelisk and the arch, the great man on his horse, what comes next? The answer has been antimonuments, countermonuments, abstract constructions, a kind of minimalism that can be overbearing deserts of no meaning to their few visitors. Some modern memorials do break through, establishing a new language that touches us. And the rest? They may be an honest reflection of our spiritual alienation, of a culture that is fragmented, but they leave us in a wilderness of broken things. They are a disappearing act.

In 1986, Jochen Gerz and Esther Shalev-Gerz built a monument meant to disappear. A city council in Hamburg, Germany, had commissioned a "Monument Against Fascism." Over the course of seven years, the column, nearly forty feet tall, slowly retracted into the ground, until there was nothing but a patch on the sidewalk. They covered the slender aluminum column, just over three feet square, with a layer of dark, soft lead. The Gerzes invited citizens to write on it with metal styluses hanging from the corners, "to add their names here to ours. In doing so, we commit ourselves to remain vigilant." They expected orderly rows of names. Photos show the dark column covered in graffiti—a banal sprawl of swastikas and Stars of David and funny faces. "The filth brings us closer to the truth than would any list of well-meaning signatures," said the local newspaper. "The inscriptions, a conglomerate of approval, hatred, anger and stupidity, are like a fingerprint of our city applied to the column." It was an eyesore whose only benefit was that it would soon disappear. That's what the Gerzes had intended. They had refused to site their memorial in a leafy, green park and deliberately chose a "normal uglyish" pedestrian mall near a dioxin dump. Their monument was a deliberate provocation. "From the beginning, the artists had intended this monument to torment—not reassure—its neighbors. They have likened it, for example, to a great black knife in the back of Germany, slowly being plunged in, each thrust solemnly commemorated by the community, a self-mutilation," said scholar James E. Young.

"What we did not want," Jochen Gerz said, "was an enormous pedestal with something on it presuming to tell people what they ought to think." That would be too much like fascism, with the monument as dictator, preempting independent thought. "Gerz makes monuments, but he hates monuments," said architect Gustavo Nielsen.

As the monument receded, it told Hamburg's citizens that they were on their own. "In the long run, it is only we ourselves who can stand up against injustice," Jochen Gerz said. There would be no hiding in art, no aspiration to grace, no uplift, no happily-ever-after moral that Germany has once more found its way. This is "perhaps the first memorial in history that does not want to be better than the society by which it is erected," said German art historian Walter Grasskamp. As I look at the pictures of this ugly, self-destroying monument, it seems to slink away from the fascist legacy it should confront. It is a small tower of Babel.

In another German city, Jochen Gerz created another disappearing act. This one started out in the ground, a buried memorial. There's nothing to be seen but a plaza of cobblestones and a sign saying. "Platz des Unsichtbaren Mahnmals: The Place of the Invisible Monument."

He created this Holocaust memorial on the sly, without permission or a commission. It was an illegal, guerrilla act of commemoration. Over several nights, his students dug up cobbles and snuck them out in their book bags. They left other cobbles in their place so the good citizens of Saarbrucken wouldn't suspect anything. Then Gerz had the cobbles inscribed with the names of the 2,146 Jewish cemeteries that existed in 1939 before the Nazis began destroying them.

Gerz chose this square because it faces the regional assembly hall, the Saarbrucken Schloss, which in World War II was the Gestapo's regional headquarters with a basement jail. Some of the prisoners managed to scratch messages and their names on the walls—their last testament—which can still be read. Almost all the Jews in the region were rounded up and sent ultimately to Auschwitz.

The students returned in darkness and installed the inscribed cobblestones—*face down*. When word spread about the students' vandalism, angry residents came to the square to see what had been done, but there was nothing to see. In that moment, they became the memorial, says James E. Young, a leading scholar of Holocaust memory. "Gerz hoped they would realize that such memory was already in them," he said. Standing there on the cobblestones, they became the monument.

The Holocaust has left an absence, and only by absence can we approach this vast loss, says Gerz. The absence is the monument. We don't stand before a great object that strains to seize our attention. Gerz says, "That same absence also allows each person to become the author of his own commemorative work."

The illegal monument, this outbreak of unsanctioned remembrance, came before the regional assembly. Some members walked out, but those who remained adopted the stealth monument, commissioning it retrospectively. They even voted to rename the Schlossplatz, the Place of the Invisible Monument.

But isn't that a sign we could put up almost anywhere? Think of all the silenced memorials you may pass in a week that are unseen, a blurred background to your daily commute: the green-mottled great man on his horse, hosting only pigeons; the curious obelisk looking like a stunted Washington Monument; the historical marker crowded with so many words it looks like a warning label written by a cadre of liability lawyers. So much narrative left out in the weather, so much storytelling that has lost its meaning.

"The invisibility of our monument was like a cure," says Gerz. But is it? We are the witnesses—unreliable, distracted, confused, in a fog of unknowing—but the only witnesses available, each of us in the empty plaza authoring a commemoration. We are the monument. But just what kind of monument are we?

At the old monuments, we walk toward the dead. We make our bid for our call to the past be answered. At the modern countermonuments, the antimonuments, no such walk is possible. The antimonument says all rituals are a lie, puppet play at the edge of the open grave. Face it: We live and die. Put away your stories, dismiss your heroes.

We have come a long way from the zinc Civil War soldier standing watch on the common, a long way from the elegant Cenotaph and Vietnam Veterans Memorial—even though some at first saw menace in its minimalism. What memorials seek is to keep the dead with us. We used to live that way. Once the living kept the dead with them, and the dead watched over the living. That's the report that anthropologists and sociologists brought back over and over from traditional cultures: Time was unbroken, time was a unity, past and present, grandmother and grandchild, were the same.

Building a monument, we reach for that lost unity. We want to say, "The dead are still with us. The great leader is with us; the war dead are with us, forever." But we are not unified. Each new monument is born amid debate: Are classical columns and wreaths appropriate? What is this expanse of poured concrete and rusty-brown Corten steel trying to tell us? With each new monument, we are really asking, "Are ancestors obsolete?"

Bunker Hill Day Parade, June 16, 2019. ALEXANDRE TZIRIPOULOFF.

A PARADE, A PICNIC, A REVOLUTION

In David Hannigan's earliest memories, he is climbing the stairs inside the Bunker Hill Monument with his father, Tommy. Up and up they go, following the 294 tightly twisting steps, big steps for a boy four or five years old.

"Was that hard?" his father asked him.

"Yes," said his son.

"Imagine how hard it was for the men fighting here," his father said.

Years later Hannigan realized how hard that climb was for his father, a veteran of World War II. "He served in the Navy and actually was badly wounded and wasn't expected to survive, wasn't expected to walk again. I didn't recognize that as a child—that my father taking us up to the top of the monument was the closest thing to witnessing a miracle. His body was shattered, but his determination was greater than his disabilities."

Tommy Hannigan wanted his son to know that "every American battle is connected to the battle fought here, and that every American who's served their country is connected to the men who fought here." This wasn't a line from a school textbook; it's what Tommy's parents, who were Irish immigrants, taught him. Tommy's parents "embraced everything that this country represented," says Hannigan. "And I know that they expected their children to only ask one thing from the country, and that is to serve and nothing else. You had to protect the country and everything that it represents, defend the Constitution, defend the liberty of this nation. And I think he was a very good teacher."

It's why David Hannigan has spent the last ten years as a National Park Service ranger at the Bunker Hill Monument in Charlestown, Massachusetts, near his own birthplace. "After my father's death, I found that this would be a good way to serve the country, and battle against historical illiteracy. It's the greatest evil."

I've met him near the monument on the Sunday before Bunker Hill Day, June 17, the 249th anniversary of the battle. The weekend's events are Charlestown's own village holiday, "Townie Christmas—the best day of the year," with a big parade, family reunions, cookouts, and presiding over it all, but at a distance like the monument on the skyline, is what is actually being celebrated.

The Battle of Bunker Hill was fierce; the losses were the worst of any battle in the Revolution. The colonists' defiance surprised King George III and impressed Europe. The king would send more men, tens of thousands of troops. The American Revolution, the fight that lasted from 1775 to 1783, started on this hill. It was "perhaps the decisive day . . . on which the fate of America depends," Abigail Adams wrote to her husband, John Adams, the day after the battle.

We have since known other decisive days, says Hannigan: December 7, 1941, or September 11, 2001—dates that mark before and after. "I try to indicate just the tragedy that was played out here in Charlestown, with hundreds and hundreds of lives being erased in a matter of minutes, the shock that is evident in statements by both British and American leadership," he says. In two hours of combat, the British suffered nearly a 50 percent casualty rate, with 1,054 soldiers killed or wounded. The New England militia lost an estimated 441 soldiers, dead, wounded, or captured.

We're standing at the Massachusetts Gate on the steps to the monument park, a small green rise corralled by elegant red-brick rowhouses. Visitors by twos and threes pause, hold up their phones, and smile for a selfie. The monument, a twenty-story obelisk, looks crisp and pure in the background. Dog walkers stop to pose their dogs (Fido on the Freedom

Trail). The neighbors are coming out, setting up chairs for the parade. The first runners in the Boys and Girls Club's Battle of Bunker Hill Road Race stream by. It's a Sunday in the park, as fine a June day as you'll ever find.

Just up the hill, thirty men were bayoneted to death. General Joseph Warren, Boston's favorite doctor, took a musket ball in the face. Warren was memorialized as the Revolution's first martyr. As the redcoats charged uphill, on their third and final assault, the militia, out of ammunition, threw rocks and swung their muskets like clubs before they retreated. The British Navy shelled Charlestown, setting it ablaze.

After the battle, British Lieutenant John Waller wrote home,

> *I cannot pretend to describe the Horror of the Scene within the Redoubt [the fort] when we enter'd it, 'twas streaming with Blood & strew'd with dead & dying Men the Soldiers stabbing some and dashing out the Brains of others was a sight too dreadful for me to dwell any longer on.*

And today? A father tosses a Frisbee to his two little girls, a family sets up a table topped by a tower of pizza boxes. One sun worshipper lays out, lizard-like. This is the other monument: A day without war.

Men died where we picnic. The peace of the park buries the dead. Small memorial flags—the Stars and Stripes and the Union Jack, one for each fallen soldier—have been set out between the paths leading to the monument. It looks like a tulip bed, a nice touch of color.

The battle here was 249 years ago, and on this sunny, breezy June day, it may as well have been in the Pleistocene, the Ice Age.

The Bunker Hill Monument was born out of a worry that, fifty years on, America was losing touch with the Revolutionary War generation, losing touch with a generation that was "united . . . in a common cause in defense of their rights," as President James Monroe said on his visit to the battlefield in 1817. Monroe was seeking to unify the country after the divisive War of 1812, a war New Englanders hated.

The monument was an ambitious undertaking: a statement that New England had led in battle and would lead in patriotic memory. The effort to remember rivaled what was being remembered. The monument took fifteen years to build. The first commercial horse-drawn railroad was built to move massive granite blocks. Work stopped repeatedly when funds ran out. For seven years it stood as a thirty-seven-foot-tall granite stump, a neighborhood eyesore. Work resumed and then stopped again for years. In debt, the Bunker Hill Monument Association sold two-thirds of the battlefield—a field they had saved from being cut into house lots.

Not everyone wanted a grand national monument. One veteran, Major Caleb Stark of New Hampshire, pleaded, "Give us bread, not granite": "In room of giving them the bread that was solemnly promised, the debt is to be paid by a stone!!" (There was no pension for veterans until 1818.) Seth Luther, a mill worker and labor leader whose father fought in the Revolution, said let it stand unfinished "until our rights are acknowledged." "The unfinished monument is a most excellent emblem of our unfinished independence." Others argued that an unadorned battlefield was the most powerful witness.

The battlefield, without the memorial, was a magnet. Marquis de Lafayette, hero of the Revolution and "guest of the nation," visited twice on his triumphal tour of America in 1824 and 1825. The Frenchman was greeted everywhere with big parades, banquets, and toasts. Temporary triumphal arches were erected for him to parade under. Temples were built out of flowers. Old veterans came forth to be greeted and embraced; Lafayette remembered their names. Congress granted him $200,000 in stock ($6.5 million today) and an entire township of land. He was the last living general from the Continental Army, the last living link to Washington. He visited Mount Vernon and tearfully entered Washington's tomb. We have no comparable heroes.

Lafayette's tour revived interest in honoring the Revolution by saving Independence Hall (it had been partially demolished, and the rest might come down) and saving the battlefields at Yorktown and Bunker Hill. His visit to Bunker Hill was emotional, said witnesses. "Sir, I tread this holy ground," said Lafayette, "where the blood of American patriots . . . early and gloriously spilled, aroused the energy of three millions, and secured the happiness of ten millions, and of many other millions of men in times to come." In Paris, Lafayette's coffin is surrounded by soil gathered from this battlefield.

To consecrate this "holy ground," Lafayette returned to lay the cornerstone for the monument, even though there was no design yet and the foundation would wait another two years. Almost one hundred thousand turned out—double Boston's population. As Lafayette rode in a long parade, his passage was marked by the crowds on the street, in windows, on roofs and chimneys, waving white handkerchiefs. Lafayette's tour had relieved the country from a fractious presidential campaign. "All the discord" was forgotten, said James Fenimore Cooper, "and nothing was thought of but Lafayette and the heroes of the Revolution."

When the monument was finally dedicated in 1843, Secretary of State Daniel Webster, the great orator, said the monument had one meaning. It stood for "one country, one constitution, and one destiny." That was the wish, that was what these Americans, in the decades before the Civil War, were trying to conjure. Webster's speech, it was said, was "household words throughout the nation."

Several days a week, hourly from 11:00 a.m. to 3:00 p.m., in front of the monument, visitors gather to hear a park ranger talk about the "decisive day." The rangers will talk to two people or two hundred. No matter. They will welcome the group by asking them where they're from and then deftly sketch the prelude to war, the costly battle, and what it all means. They will set out a battlefield map and a map showing the shoreline of colonial Boston. Talking for just a few minutes, they will build a timeline, introduce some leaders of the militia, and conclude by pointing the way to the years of fighting to come.

Day after day they build the monument. They do what the seven thousand tons of granite piled up in the obelisk can't do: They tell a story.

"My grandparents came from Ireland," says Hannigan, "and a saying in Ireland is, The dead are only dead if we stop talking about them."

The monument's designer got in the first—and really the last—word on his design. Horatio Greenough was a twenty-year-old Harvard student when he submitted his entry for the competition to design the monument. Among the fifty entries, there were many towering classical columns and columns with urns. Greenough chose an obelisk, an Egyptian form considered the proper way to proclaim the eternal memory of the dead. Greenough would go on to study in Italy, becoming America's first sculptor. (His Washington statue, exposing the Founding Father's torso, was scandalous.)

His design, as built, is spare—there are no names, no laurels in stone, no urns, no statues or busts. The monument association considered adding names, but decided that plain stone was a better collective tribute: All the soldiers, living and dead, were united in one cause, the new republic, *out of many, one.*

Greenough said, "The obelisk has to my eye a singular aptitude in its form and character to call attention to a spot memorable in history. It says but one word, but it speaks loud. If I understand its voice, it says, Here! It says no more." The Bunker Hill Monument just marks the spot—*Here.* It doesn't tell us what to think or even offer a line of narrative. The story of Bunker Hill and the Revolution has to be earned, in each generation, just as David Hannigan's father taught him, step by step.

PART II

"EVERYTHING IN THE PAST IS ALWAYS WAITING, WAITING TO DETONATE."

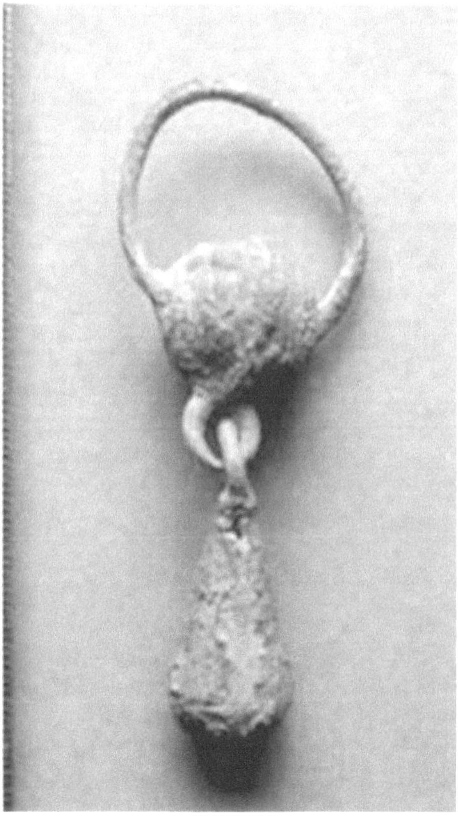

This silver pendant was worn as a necklace. It was found buried with a child, age three and a half to five and a half, known now only as Burial 254 in Manhattan's African Burial Ground. FROM ARCHAEOLOGICAL REPORTS.

WALKING ON THE DEAD

Two New Yorkers, each known only by a number:

Burial 6: A man, twenty-five to thirty years old, maybe one of the Fulbe in what is now Benin in West Africa. One of his teeth is filed, a common custom. He was buried with five buttons, two of which have anchors. He may have been in the British Navy, or he may have found the buttons. His skeleton shows a life of hard labor: arthritis in his arms, legs, and back from carrying heavy loads, some balanced on his head. There are many small fractures in his neck bones. He probably had rickets and was anemic from too little iron in his diet. He would have felt tired all the time. His swollen, arthritic joints hurt. "This man's ailments and injuries were common among the enslaved Africans in New York, and so was his early death," say historians.

Burial 25: A woman, aged about twenty-two, with a "blunt force fracture of her lower face." Her right arm was twisted and pulled, breaking the bone. There is a musket ball, a half-inch round, beneath her ribs. She was probably shot in the back or side, a rare violent death.

These old bones have power. When a backhoe struck a coffin, revealing a skull, everything stopped. A thirty-four-story office building was halted. The foreman was called over. He called his boss, who called other bosses, who called in the archaeologists, who arrived like a bomb-disposal squad. They gently probed with small gardening-sized trowels, brushes as small as a toothbrush, and dental picks. They brought forth an old Manhattan map, long forgotten, one that says, "Negros Burial Ground."

The first burials were in the late seventeenth century. Here lie enslaved Africans, barred from the White churches' graveyards, buried beyond the city wall—the stockade they built—a ten-minute walk from where they may have been bought and sold at the municipal slave market on Wall Street. No church consecrated these grounds. A year after the grounds were full and the burials stopped, the hills nearby were leveled. The dirt was piled on to the old graves, in places twenty-five feet deep, and the old graveyard was cut up into house lots.

The archaeologists uncovered Burial 6, Burial 25, and hundreds of others. There may be fifteen thousand graves, maybe more, maybe twenty thousand laid to rest on about six and a half acres. But most of what they found were coffin nails and the copper pins that held a shroud over a body. Mostly the bones have returned to the earth. The coffins were only dark outlines in the Manhattan soil. Gone. Fifteen thousand or twenty thousand lives, and not one name is known to us.

In cities and towns, the dead have more addresses than we want to acknowledge. Going about our day, grabbing a coffee on the way to work, dropping off dry cleaning, striding along on a fine spring day, we are walking on the dead.

"Underneath America lies an apartheid of the departed. Violence done to the living is usually done to their dead, who are dug up, mowed down, and built on," said historian Jill Lepore. Underneath us lies the history we refuse to acknowledge. "Everything in the past is always waiting, waiting to detonate," said the great architectural historian, Vincent Scully.

A backhoe hits bones, an old map comes to light, the past detonates. The bones speak.

Burial 101: A man in his early thirties with filed teeth, signs of tropical disease, bowing of a thigh bone, and fractured vertebrae. "His forced labors were backbreaking in the literal sense," says an archaeologist. The lid of his coffin is decorated with brass tacks in a heart-shaped symbol that may be a Sankofa, a West African heart-shaped symbol that counsels the living to look to the past for guidance.

The bones were found in 1991 during the construction of a federal office building. The environmental-impact statement said that the new building would stand on part of the old burial ground, but no one thought they would find any remains. Archaeologists, hired to check, investigated an alley that had never been built on. They thought they might find a grave or two. They found 100 graves, then it was 200, and by the time they stopped, 419 graves. There may be another 200 graves in that alley. They had uncovered the earliest and largest African American graveyard and maybe the largest from the colonial period for any group.

With the bones came the past, the buried story of Northern slavery. The Dutch brought the first enslaved Africans to New Amsterdam in 1626, eleven young men from the Congo and Angola regions. By the end of their tenure in 1664, about 40 percent of New Amsterdam's population was African. They built the city. They farmed; built houses, ships, and city streets; unloaded cargo at the wharves. They drilled with the Dutch militia and baptized their children in the Dutch Reformed Church. The enslaved could own property; they could choose their owners. They had a legal standing in the courts. When eleven men and their wives petitioned for their freedom in 1644, the town council freed them and gave them land to farm—poor land rejected by White farmers—but they had their freedom. ("Half-freedom," the Dutch called it. The adults had to pay an annual tribute to the Dutch; their children were still enslaved. The Dutch set up the half-free beyond the city walls to act as a buffer from the native Lenape.)

The English followed and instituted stricter laws—curfews, bans against gatherings of more than four slaves, bans against assembling at night (the customary time for funerals), punishment without trial. Passes were required to travel more than a mile. Land couldn't be inherited, extinguishing the farms that had begun under the Dutch. The enslaved rose up in 1712, killing nine Whites and injuring about a dozen others. Twenty-three men were executed: hanged, burned alive, starved to death, or "broken alive upon a wheel." Another "conspiracy" followed in 1741. Seventeen Blacks were hanged, thirteen were burned at the stake, and they were buried in the Negros Burial Ground. At the start of the Revolution, only Charleston, South Carolina, had more slaves.

The discovery of the burials remade the map—slave market, city walls, burial grounds. It's not your usual New York tour. There's a story that New York loves to tell about itself—the city that never sleeps, the Big Apple, "a-number-one, top-of-the-heap," come here and make it big—but this a different story: Slavery in the North, hard lives, segregation, burial, neglect, and desecration. The dead lying forgotten under city streets, in basements, under towering piles of dirt heaped on them.

Burial 323: A man, nineteen to thirty years old, buried without a coffin "under inauspicious circumstances" after "postmortem surgery." The top of his skull was sawn off, possibly during a coroner's inquest or by medical students who raided the graveyard so often the African American community petitioned the city council to stop them. He was buried hugging the top of his skull to his chest.

To the builders, the bones were an obstacle, threatening contracts and delivery dates. To archaeologists, the bones were information—the only testimony left about who these people were, the only way for the nameless to speak. The bosses and their bosses wanted to resume work as quickly as possible. They rushed the archaeologists to work eleven-hour days, seven days a week, and produce a report so they could get concrete and steel into the ground. The bosses promised that there would be a memorial, a display, a plaque, something appropriate.

They exhumed 419 burials and sent them to be studied. Approximately 40 percent were infants. About two hundred graves were left to study. The archaeologists work until the Black community rises up and says, Enough. Those are my ancestors' bones: *"Some of them bones is my mother's bones come together for to rise and shine. Some of them bones is my father's bones. Some of them bones is mine,"* they say, quoting an African American spiritual. Those bones belong to us. They're family; they're sacred. Let them rest.

Sherrill Wilson, an urban anthropologist and an expert on African Americans in colonial New York, knows the importance of the archaeologists' work. Wilson was the director of the Office of Public Education and Interpretation for the African Burial Ground Project. Her job was to tell the story of slavery in New York, but the bones stopped her, too. When she dug up the brittle femur of a boy, "I felt like, 'This is my child.' I was like Lady Macbeth. I couldn't wash him off, and then I didn't wash my hand for some time. I realized that when you touch these bones, you get a person, not a scientific specimen, and I just couldn't do it anymore."

Burial 340: A woman, middle-aged, with 112 glass beads that she wore around her waist, most blue, a few yellow, one black, and cowry shells. These beads were used as currency in West Africa. She may have been "a healer or a ritual leader in her community."

As quickly as the burial ground had been discovered, it was disappearing again, part of the big city's churn, with taller buildings replacing earlier ones and millions of lives erasing earlier lives. Day by day the city writes over the previous days and years. To the Black community, their ancestors, who had been discarded, were being swiftly obliterated once more.

They were outraged. They watched as construction continued and bones and coffin nails were dug up, mapped, wrapped, and trucked off to a lab. When a backhoe digging one of the footings for the foundation struck and destroyed twenty graves, they had reached their limit. In angry community meetings, in a twenty-six-hour "remembrance vigil" attended by thousands, in a petition with more than one hundred thousand signatures, they said, Stop the digging; stop the building. We don't want some plaque in the lobby of an office building; we want respect. How dare you offer us a plaque. Why are we having all these meetings? You haven't listened to us. Stop. We must preserve and honor these graves.

They came to worship; they made offerings of food to their ancestors. *Them bones is our bones.* They took their case to Congress and won. Part of Public Law 102-393 "immediately" halted archaeological excavation and construction of part of the building. The African Burial Ground National Monument would take the place of a planned four-story atrium. There would be a museum in the office building. The remains were transferred to Howard University for further study, where their arrival was honored with a candlelight vigil and an "Ancestral Tribute." For their return, all 419 remains were placed in hand-carved mahogany coffins from Ghana. A representative set of remains, four coffins, made a six-day journey up the East Coast. "The Rites of Ancestral Return" was celebrated in Washington, Baltimore, Wilmington, Philadelphia, Newark, and New York. A New Jersey police motorboat carried the coffins to the Wall Street pier, near the slave market, where they were received with prayers, songs, drumming, and speeches before they arrived at the burial ground to be reinterred under seven earthen mounds by a new monument, an Ancestral Chamber that looks like a tent-shaped granite shelter. Maya Angelou spoke at the ceremonies: "You may bury me in the bottom of Manhattan. I will rise. My people will get me. I will rise out of the huts of history's shame."

This national monument is the opposite of the Gerzes' disappearing Hamburg monument retracting inch by inch into the ground. This site is a rising, the bones bringing a renewal to the living. The bones come together to rise and shine, as the spiritual "Dem Bones," or "Dry Bones," says. The prophet Ezekiel enters the Valley of Dry Bones. God commands Ezekiel to preach to the bones, to listen to the word of God, and they will return to life: "So I prophesied as he commanded me, and breath entered them; they came to life and stood up on their feet—a vast army."

This is why we erect memorials. We want the bones to live, but we'll settle for a living memory. Anthropologist Michael Blakely, who was the director of the African Burial Ground Project, understands this. "What does it mean to be human? What would be on the final exam of an introductory course?" he asked. He ran through the usual list, including using tools and fire. But "what marks the earliest *homo sapiens* is the burial of the dead. Ultimately, it is to imagine the continuing social obligations of human beings, even to the dead. I sometimes think that we should be called *homo reminiscens*, not *sapiens*, that what distinguishes us is that we are the memorializers."

Burial 254: A child, aged three and a half to five and a half, found with a cast-silver pendant that was worn as a necklace. "You know," said Blakely, "there's one example of a silver ear bob that a child had worn, that was placed around a child's neck as a pendant, by people who were desperately poor as the enslaved of New York. They gave that to that child."

Three days after the reburial ceremonies in New York, in the small city of Portsmouth, New Hampshire, a backhoe struck a coffin. They were digging into a street for a sewer manhole. Work stopped; archaeologists were called. The archaeologists had warned the workers that they were on the site of Portsmouth's "Negro Burying Yard." The coffins were in a shallow grave, some less than eighteen inches below. They mapped the coffins—there were twenty-six—locating them on a photo of the street.

In the photo, the coffins are gray silhouettes—absences made visible—imposed on the rumpled asphalt of a city street. There are houses alongside, telephone poles and wires. Just another day, except—what are these coffins doing here?

The coffins are adrift, loose on some unseen tide, but here they are on Chestnut Street. The coffins litter the street and sidewalk, with the classic tapered shape, heads facing west. They look like they've been dumped, fallen off the back of a truck, forgotten, built over, and built through. At a presentation about the burial ground, there was a gasp when everyone saw this image—the dead as litter. No one wants to be discarded. No one wants to admit that we walk on the dead.

The coffins were buried here starting in 1705. Before the Revolution, Portsmouth was a thriving port, like New York City, profiting from the labor of enslaved Africans and a few free Blacks, who were about 4 percent of the population. "New Englanders were the colonial leaders in the slave trade as shipbuilders, shippers, and merchants who bought and sold enslaved Africans," says historian Marc Howard Ross. Profits from the slave trade built Ivy League colleges; Southern cotton fed the Northern mills. Today most people, says another historian, have "no idea there were ever slaves in the North."

The New Hampshire Constitution in 1783 declared that all men "were born equal and independent." Slavery was outlawed six years later, but it lingered, with some remaining slaves in the state, until a few years before the Civil War. The burying yard was abandoned around 1800, and the city forgot about its African Americans—call it a calculated carelessness, a curated blindness. "It's convenient to *not* see what you don't want to see," said Valerie Cunningham, a pioneering "truth teller" whose lifelong dedication brought forth New Hampshire's Black Heritage Trail.

The city grew up and then over the burial ground. With the jail nearby, it "made a kind of Golgotha of that then neglected part of town," said a local newspaper. Workmen putting in a gas line in 1853 "disturbed numerous remains," including a coffin "containing the bones of a large and tall man." They reburied him and returned to work. Later in the century, or in the early twentieth century, a clay sewer pipe was pushed right through several graves. In all, as many as two hundred graves may be underneath this short street and nearby, under houses, parking lots, and other streets.

The archaeologists studied eight remains and left the others in the ground. Only the teeth were left in most burials; a few others had teeth and long bones. They spent five hundred hours in the lab, extracting teeth and bones from the clay soil. The average age of the dead was twenty years old—half that of their White neighbors. Two had filed teeth. One child (Burial 7), aged seven to twelve years old, was buried above an adult male (Burial 12). "In one instance (Burial 2), the skeleton was nearly complete, except for the cranium—apparently destroyed by the backhoe when excavating the hole for the sewer manhole." Their names are unknown.

The mayor convened a committee, and over the course of a dozen years, they hired a landscape architect and an artist and closed Chestnut Street to create the African Burial Ground Memorial Park. It's a crowded memorial with three "zones" in one short block. The entry is flanked by two bronze statues, one representing the city's first enslaved African, and the other, "Mother Africa." They stand on opposite sides of a granite slab and reach around, their hands not touching. A red-granite serpentine path runs through the park. "The Petition Line" is inscribed with the words from twenty Portsmouth slaves who petitioned the New Hampshire legislature for their freedom in 1779. This line leads to the burial vault, which has a circular lid decorated with a Sankofa. The eight remains that were removed for study were wrapped in white cloth with red ribbons, placed in new coffins with small gifts of shells, coins, beads, poems, prayers, and a toy for the one child. They were reburied in a ceremony led by Chief Oscar Ogugua Mokeme, a Nigerian-born cultural leader, mixing his native Igbo with English and blowing on an elephant tusk (*ebe okuko*) to offer a prayer.

The Sankofa is encircled by flat bronze figures meant to represent the "collective modern community of Portsmouth come together to witness the site's history and protect the remains." Each figure is inscribed with a line of a poem by the artist, "We Stand in Honor of Those Forgotten." Behind them is a granite wall topped with a railing "based on an African Kente cloth motif suggestive of boat paddles." The railing holds ceramic tiles in the Kente style made by middle school students. The park also has information panels.

This is an add-a-thing memorial. They told a story and another story. It's a casserole of ideas rather than one clear image, as in the Cenotaph and the Vietnam Veterans Memorial. Do visitors make an emotional connection, do they understand the history? Maybe. Most of the comments that visitors leave online are respectful, saying the burial ground is "sobering" and "moving," a polite response to a polite memorial. But there are also comments like this one: "Worth a few minutes of your time if you are walking around Portsmouth. Nice to see the acknowledgment of the bad things from the past with the hope that we will do better in the future." Nice. Good for us to do this. Now, time for lunch.

At the first public meeting, when they broke into smaller focus groups to review the early designs, some were concerned that the memorial would be just another nice park. They said this memorial should be "not picnic-y, a little uncomfortable, get to the hardship, create a sense of absence, not too majestic." But creating a memorial that confronts and upsets visitors without driving them off is challenging. You could say that this is the design brief for Holocaust memorials. Visitors are asked to be witnesses, to stare into the abyss. But how much truth telling can any of us accept?

The bones are the memorial. The reburial ceremonies are the memorial. Whatever we build above ground can't approach the power of a skull or a femur or rib cage sticking out from the dirt. The nameless dead have a claim on us.

Four years after Portsmouth dedicated the African Burial Ground Memorial Park, on Florida's Gulf Coast in Tampa, archaeologists, prompted by the *Tampa Bay Times*, found 126 coffins under the public housing of Robles Park Village and at least 55 more graves next door under the parking lot for Sunstate Wrecker, Tampa's "premier provider of heavy-duty towing." They were just getting started. The apartments, the big wreckers, and another warehouse had buried Zion Cemetery, one of Tampa's first for Blacks. Using ground-penetrating radar, archaeologist Rebecca O'Sullivan and her staff found about three hundred graves, four to six feet deep, on the apartment grounds. Back in her office, when O'Sullivan loaded the scans into her computer, "it popped up on my screen, and . . . seeing these shapes that are the exact shape, size, depth of a coffin, it really was like a punch to the gut to see that." Mapping the site, they superimposed the coffins over a photo of Robles Park Village, lines of blue boxes all over the courtyards, "right up to, next to people's porches." But still, there were missing graves: nearly eight hundred death certificates list the two and a half acres of Zion Cemetery.

Founded in 1901, Zion Cemetery disappeared from city maps in the 1920s. Tampa taxed the cemetery, even though cemeteries were tax exempt, and the land returned to the original White owners. The land was sold in 1926; all references to the cemetery were expunged from the property record, and the gravestones were removed. A chicken farm, the Blue Moon Poultry shop, and a few homes replaced Zion, completing the land grab.

Tampa took the chicken farm/cemetery and more land by eminent domain in 1951 to build Whites-only public housing, evicting a long-established Black community near Robles Pond. The community objected, but they were not heard. "A letter from several Negroes . . . protesting the construction" has been received, say the minutes of the Tampa Bay Housing Authority. They didn't respond; they couldn't even be bothered to name the letter writers.

Three children's coffins were unearthed during construction. Work paused briefly. The city claimed that all the graves had been removed. No one dug for more graves, and work resumed. By the mid-1960s, most residents of Robles Park Village were Black, and sixty years later, it was time to evict the residents. Tampa planned to tear down the apartments for a new mix of "affordable housing." Residents could return—if they met a high threshold: They needed to earn 80 percent of the local median income.

"They always say that," said Yvette Lewis, president of the local branch of the NAACP. "Honestly, they don't want Black folks—common Black folks—to live over there. They want to develop that into a beautiful piece of land that White people will reap the benefits off our misery and suffering. So they are just hurt, and they're upset that they found a cemetery."

As the city was emptying the apartments, the past came calling, with more graves found each week. You could say that Zion Cemetery reappeared. Lewis took in the news. "First I was in disbelief, and I was like, 'No, it just really can't be true,'" she said. "You know, then I was in shock. You go through all of the emotions."

Tampa continued building, setting aside part of the land for a memorial. They put up a historical marker and began to debate how to remember. A park would be nice, with walking trails. "These people have been walked on all their lives, and now they want to rest, and people still want to walk on them," Lewis said.

With Zion in the news, people called the *Tampa Bay Times* to report other erased Black cemeteries, the way in other places people might tally bear sightings:

- There was a paupers' graveyard (primarily Black) at a high school. As many as 267 had been buried there; ground-penetrating radar found more than half of the burials. The school put up a fence.
- On land that had once belonged to a Baptist church, there were at least seventy graves. They thought they had moved all the graves when the church closed, but many were left behind. They are now under an office building and a parking lot.
- Another site is a vacant lot engulfed by a large Italian Club Cemetery; another, on the local air force base; another, at a house museum on plantation land; and another, on a horse ranch. A forensic anthropologist from the University of South Florida has identified forty-five unmarked or forgotten burial grounds in Tampa.

In France, there are crews dedicated to defusing unexploded bombs, mostly from the two World Wars, but sometimes they are called to retrieve artillery shells from the Franco-Prussian War, and that was in 1870. More than a century after World War I, there are twelve million artillery shells in the soil around Verdun in France and millions more around Marne and Somme. French *demineurs* were busy in the 1990s with two million calls from citizens to pick up unexploded bombs. The "iron harvest" is steady work. They remove nine hundred tons each year; it will take at least five hundred years to clear the bombs.

Farmers, working fields that have been declared safe, have pulled shells out of the furrows they have ploughed and left them by the roadside. The earth keeps forcing up shells, the unending harvest of war, sometimes killing farmers. (Thirty-six died in 1991, but death is much rarer today.) "Their harvesters can't distinguish a hand grenade from a potato, a mortar from a beet," writes Donovan Webster.

A *demineur*, leaving a garden where they had removed two World War II tank shells from a stone wall, assessed his job: "Only the usual story. The soldiers moved on. The war moved on. The bombs stayed."

In cities and towns, we are walking on hidden history; we are walking on the dead. You'd expect that in Rome or London, but it's usually a surprise to Americans. We think that we walk free of history, each of us an American Adam, self-made, self-improving, in control of our destiny. We're surprised when the past detonates.

Desecrated African American burial grounds are not unusual. "Mortuary apartheid" is the rule. There may be three thousand abandoned cemeteries in Florida, says one state senator. One of them in St. Petersburg, Oaklawn Cemetery, was closed and condemned by the city in 1926. Today part of Oaklawn is under a parking lot at a baseball stadium—VIP Lot 1 at Tropicana Field, home to the Tampa Bay Rays until Hurricane Milton tore the roof off. Move up the East Coast, and the story is the same. There are a hundred or more—no one knows: one under a neighborhood in Charleston, another under a highway in Durham, another under a shopping center in Baltimore, another under a playground in Philadelphia, and another under a bus depot in Harlem.

Black history is hidden everywhere. It's even in Section 27 of Arlington National Cemetery, which holds the first burials, including 3,639 "Freedmen," slaves emancipated in the Civil War and 1,500 "U.S. Colored Troops" who fought for the Union. They have a hidden cohort, the unmarked graves of the Africans enslaved by Robert E. Lee and his father-in-law when Arlington was a plantation. "Enslaved people molded the land there, buried their dead, and made claims to the place and their own histories within it. Their sweat, blood, and tears had already sanctified that ground long before 1864," when Arlington became a national military cemetery, says historian Micki McElya.

Arlington began as an African burial ground. More Black graveyards are being uncovered each year. Each one demands that we reckon with the past. The past detonates again and again. These are your buried bombs, America.

Burial 335: A woman, about thirty years old, with a newborn sheltered under her right arm (Burial 356). She may have been born in West Africa, or she descended from people who were. Growing up, she was malnourished. She had arthritis in her spine from heavy lifting.

The Cheshire, a streamlined train, passing through the Summit Cut in March 1951.

WHEN THE WAR BETWEEN THE CORKONIANS AND FAR DOWNS CAME TO AMERICA

I. "Name Unknown"

The brief newspaper reports are casual: Four or five Irish killed. Some Irish killed. The Irish were railroad workers and canal builders in the 1830s and later, in this strange new land only a few years. A man or two would be blown up blasting rocks with gunpowder or in an unspecified accident digging a canal ditch. This might earn a line or two in the local newspapers. The men were never named. There were no follow-up reports, no accident investigations, no funeral coverage, no appeals to help the widows. Being killed on the job was not unusual. Twenty-five percent of railroad construction workers died at work, a rate three times higher than for other trades of the era.

Building a railroad near Keene, New Hampshire, far from their home in County Cork, they left the earth with little notice. "We hear . . . that four Irishmen were instantly killed on the 12th section of the 2nd division of the Cheshire Railroad on Monday last, by the falling of the bank. The contractor, Mr. Wells, narrowly escaped. The men were buried four feet deep," the *New Hampshire Sentinel* reported on January 4, 1846. And, "An Irishman (name unknown) we understand was lately killed on the

18th section of Cheshire R.R., by blasting, the charge going off when he was tamping [down the gunpowder]," the paper reported in June 1847. Five lines of type for the four buried Irishmen; four lines for an exploded Irishman. Each man is anonymous. These reports were rare. Most deaths went unreported.

The death notice for the Irishman killed by a blast of gunpowder and a rain of rocks appeared alongside four other brief death notices, all with names: Mrs. Merriam Willey, age sixty-seven; Mrs. Eliza Ann Townsend, wife of Mr. Chas. T., "after a protracted sickness," age thirty-four; Mrs. Sally Jones, age seventy, "at the poor house." And "A Mr. Mellen of Swanzey, found in the graveyard in Peterboro, with a jug of rum by his side, nearly dead. He survived but a short time after he was found." Even a widow at the poor house and a drunkard had their names said publicly, possibly for the last time.

When twenty-one Irish railroad workers were brought into court in Keene to be charged with rioting, they were at last named in the court record. In the newspaper they were only "a whole herd of Irishmen." The local town histories, written seventy and more years later, are just as careless. "Numerous assaults as well as crimes were committed among the men, but we have no details, nor do we know that they took place within our township," says one history. Thirty or more are buried in unmarked graves, but again, we don't know. They passed into the town histories as hearsay. They were here and gone. Rumors had longer lives.

This is how I first met the Irish who had come to my corner of New Hampshire. They were nameless casualties of the push to build the Cheshire Railroad.

Researching another story, reading the tight confines of the old newspapers, they appeared here and there, dead Irishmen noted in a line or two, and in a flash in one report of a riot in 1848. Hundreds of men fought at close range, firing at each other. One man was dead, two wounded. One group overran the other, destroying their shanties, smashing everything, stealing whatever cash they found. The militia was sent out from Keene, about eight miles away, arriving hours too late. All was quiet; the attackers were hiding in the woods. "Serious Affray," said the *Sentinel*'s headline. The story was only five inches long, about four hundred words.

And the next week, what did the *Sentinel* report? Nothing. And every week after that? Nothing. This was, as far as I knew, the biggest incident of labor strife in the history of Northern New England, and yet the riot appeared to be as fleeting as an apparition. I had to find out more. First, I had to look to Ireland.

When the Irish left for America—and they left by the hundreds of thousands even before the Great Famine—they left the hearth and the countryside. They left a tightly bound world, a known world in which they had traveled but a dozen miles from home in their lifetimes.

By the hearth, with its turf fire constantly tended, they visited at night, holding back the darkness with tall tales, memories of long-gone neighbors, riddles, "craic," and "guesses." They passed the fiddle to play tunes they all knew. They talked and drank, new arrivals picking up the stories as other neighbors were seen off with a short farewell: "Safe home."

The hearth was the center of the countryside. "From the hearth, the house expands to form the farm. Farm becomes community," says Henry Glassie, a scholar of folkways from the states. Glassie spent eleven years by the hearths of a small Ulster community, visiting all 153 Irish souls living in four square miles. "The community weaves stories around the central fire, weaves time and the generations." The hearth is the "crucible of continuity," he says. "A turf fire demands constant attention." It is the "kitchen's metronome."

Leaving for America extinguished the fire; leaving broke time. "Time flows through the hearth," says Glassie. When the fire dims, time itself stops. Family and friends might hold an "emigrant wake" or "America wake," a keening for their loss. The emigrants were usually never seen again.

They left a land of hardship, pushed by absentee, sometimes cruel English landlords. Several hundred families owned most of Ireland. Their big estates enclosed land that had been held in common, taking more and more tillage for cattle. There was no land to rent; there was little to eat. They had to tithe the English Protestant church. They were Catholic. (Eighty percent of the population was Catholic, ruled by the Protestant minority.) Leaving was hardship; beyond lay more hardship. They crossed the ocean, forty to forty-five days at sea. On some ships, they were treated as "paying ballast," packed into holds now empty of tobacco, cotton, or timber. On the worst ships, one-third aboard would perish.

They joined their countrymen in Philadelphia, Boston, New York, and Chicago, taking what work they could, traveling to new dots on the map. America was distance without end. "Had I fallen from the clouds amongst this people, I could not feel more isolated, more bewildered," said one. "This is a fast country. We can scarcely keep pace with it," said another. And a third said, "We are a primitive people wandering wildly in a strange land, the 19th Century."

In New York City's first Catholic newspaper, the *Truth Teller*, or Boston's leading Catholic paper, *The Boston Pilot*, they advertised seeking lost kin:

> *Of JOHN CARMODY, who left Ireland 15 years ago and landed in Quebec. He lived in the county Limerick, parish of Manister, townland of Gurrane. When last heard from, about 9 years ago, he was in the State of Pennsylvania. Any information respecting him will be thankfully received by his brothers, William and Thomas Carmody, Keene, Cheshire County, New Hampshire.*

> *Of DANIEL LOFTUS, a native of parish of Kilfine, barony of Tyrawley, co. Mayo. When last heard from he was at work for Boody & Stone, on the Cheshire Railroad, in August, '47. Any information of him will be thankfully received by his father, Andrew Loftus, Alder Creek, N.Y.*

Ireland was a memory and a longing. They were far from the hearth. "A house is sad—they say it looks lonesome—without a fire," says Glassie. "When its hearth grows cold, the heart of the house ceases to beat, the couples will fall, the walls crumble, thatch will mound in on the floor. . . . A cold hearth is a symbol of despair."

The Irish immigrants hovered near invisibility. They appeared in the press and in books as the drunken Irish; the rioting, fighting Irish; the lawless brawling buffoons; the dangerous, disgraceful, dirty, depraved, indolent, ignorant, wrong-headed, wild Irish. The word *Irish* seldom appeared without a pejorative. In the nineteenth century, *Irish* meant *Catholic*. The Protestant Irish already here started calling themselves Scots Irish when the Catholic rabble began to arrive in great numbers.

"In the name of God, do we want *these* people here?" asked the anti-immigrant nativists in 1839. They did not want "these locust legions of Irish immigrants." The nativists hated the Irish. They were taking jobs; they were voting. "Had I the power, I would erect a GALLONS [*sic*] upon every wharf in the city of New York, and HANG EVERY D—D [Damned] IRISHMAN as fast as they come on shore," said the editor of the *New York Courier and Enquirer*.

The Irish, in flight from the Great Hunger, were no more welcome at the start of their crossing, most often in Liverpool, England, a city of misery. Each year migrants arrived in Liverpool in numbers that matched the city's total population, a shadow city of suffering. Liverpool was overrun by hungry dockside beggars—"men with gallows in their eyes" and frail mothers holding up frail babies—by refugees in rags, by typhus and dysentery, by suicides, mercy killings, and madness. Corpses, retrieved from the river, were displayed naked, in view of the street, for possible identification in the "Drowned House."

Nathaniel Hawthorne, well known for popular novels like *The Scarlet Letter*, arrived in Liverpool as the American consul in 1853. He surveyed the scene: "The people are as numerous as maggots in cheese; you behold them, disgusting, and all moving about, as when you raise a plank or log that has long lain on the ground, and find many vivacious bugs and insects beneath it."

In America, the Irish consigned to the roughest work, digging canals and building railroads, and were condemned for their working conditions. James Buckingham, a British traveler, was overwhelmed by a "repulsive" work camp along the Illinois and Michigan Canal: "I never saw anything approaching to the scene before us, in dirtiness and disorder. . . . Whisky and tobacco seemed the chief delights of the men; and of the women and children, no language could give an adequate idea of their filthy condition, in garments and person." Buckingham's report was a standard issue, common enough that it reads like he was just filling in the blanks of a routine dismissal.

A priest who was sent to the workers digging the Illinois and Michigan Canal despaired. Father John Blaisius Raho was born in Naples and came to America in his midtwenties. He held mass in a nearby city and tried to keep the warring factions of the Irish canal workers apart. "They beat and kill their own countrymen; they destroy houses and crops. . . . They are extremely depraved and untouched by the grace of God," he wrote to his bishop. "I am fatigued, I am tired. Would wish to be among the Indians."

Contempt is the only thing that lifted the Irish immigrants from invisibility.

Not only were the Irish hated, but they hated each other. The Irish arrived in America not as the Irish we know, with that "wearing of the green" national pride, but as men and women from their counties, from County Cork—Corkonians—or County Longford or County Mayo—dismissed as "Far Downs" by the Corkonians. They arrived in fiercely local bands. In the growing mill city of Lowell, Massachusetts, a "Corkonian considered an emigrant from Tyrone as foreign as the Yankees who lived around both of them," says historian Brian C. Mitchell. The first Catholic church, St. Patrick's, was carefully situated between the Corkonians' and Far Downs' separate "Paddy camps." One of the leaders of the Irish asked the town fathers for constables on Sundays to ward off fighting next to the church. The divisive Paddy camps, marked by rioting, led to the unusual establishment of a second parish nearby just ten years later.

And when they were mistreated by their bosses, cheated out of pay, subjected to brutal work, or injured, they rose up—against each other. They brought their feuds with them across the ocean, carrying their "provincial spleen," as one Irishman said. They attacked and killed their fellow countrymen. "Cork men murdering Connaught men, in a strange land! What an infernal vitality the curse of Ireland has," said the *Boston Pilot*. "We are miserably disgraced."

County Cork, the largest of Ireland's thirty-two counties, was in the south, and the Far Downs, confusingly, came from the northern counties, four of which made up the province of Connaught (or Connacht). Far Downs, says one historian, is derived from *Fear aduain* in Irish, meaning *stranger*. New Yorkers first encountered the epithet when rival Irish gangs constructing the Croton Water Works in 1838 battled for control of the project, swinging pickaxes. One Corkonian was killed. After that, 150 Corkonians descended on the boarding shanty of the Far Downs, who fought back until the police and guards from the nearby Sing Sing Prison arrived.

What is the meaning of "Fardonian?" the *New York Morning Herald* asked its readers. It is an insult by the Corkonians, they concluded. "They love each other as Satan loves holy water," said a reader.

Pitched battles broke out almost every place the Irish were building canals or railroads. They hated each other with a vehemence that shocked and confused observers. On the Illinois and Michigan Canal, they clashed five times in seven years. Some riots were sparked by the Panic of 1837, when wages were cut by nearly 25 percent or were not paid. In one incident, nearly four hundred Irish workers tore through the countryside twelve miles south of Chicago, "destroying all the property within their reach, . . . threatening to take the lives of the people in the vicinity." Another time, five hundred Corkonians, armed with rifles and sharp sticks, defeated the Far Downs, seized a ferryboat, and burned all the Far Downs' dwellings, before celebrating their victory through the night. The Far Downs returned in the morning, backed by the well-armed sheriff and his posse of eighty angry locals. Ten Corkonians were killed, some shot dead as they jumped in the river. In Chicago, Far Downs assaulted a reverend who was seeking a reprieve for two Corkonians who were sentenced to hang. The despondent Father Raho gave up. He was forced to hold separate masses for Corkonians and Far Downs.

The Corkonians and Far Downs had left a violent land that was in constant rebellion, a land ruled in some counties by a "standing army of the disaffected" who raided at night, burned houses, assassinated landlords, destroyed crops, and tortured anyone who hesitated to join their campaigns. These "moonlighters" or "midnight legislators" were bound by oaths in secret societies known as the Whiteboys, Rockites, Carders, Threshers, Terry Alts, and many others. They were, at times, the law in the countryside.

"Every decade between 1760 and 1840 was punctuated by at least one major outbreak of rural discontent," say historians Samuel Clark and James S. Donnely Jr. "Parts of Ireland effectively rejected English rule," says historian Patrick O'Farrell. The kings' judges needed military escorts. Crimes committed by mobs conveniently had no witnesses. The authorities listed twenty-two categories of "rural outrage" and "agrarian outrage" (among them murder, firing at a person, attacking a house, maiming cattle, and sending threatening notices). If an arrest was made, no one would testify. It was said that some witnesses did hang themselves rather than go to court. The landlords, judges, and office holders were Protestant. "There's little use in going to law with the devil when the court is held in hell," said a Kilkenny schoolmaster.

The English, who occupied Ireland, believed the Irish were inferior, uncivilized, prone to violence, and, as Catholics, on the wrong side of the Protestant Reformation. In the seventeenth and early eighteenth centuries, the Catholic majority was barred from holding public office, voting in parliamentary elections, and joining the military. Owning land was restricted; weapons were confiscated. Catholic schools were outlawed, and the clergy was exiled. It was a "machine . . . well fitted for the oppression, impoverishment, and degradation of a people," said the statesman Edmund Burke. Seeking control, the British Parliament repeatedly studied the "Irish questions." From 1810 to 1833, there were 114 royal commissions and 60 select committees. They never addressed the basic problem: Several hundred English families owned most of Ireland. And very few English landlords actually visited Ireland.

The Irish were fighting for land, fighting for their economic survival. One of the earliest and most extensive secret societies, the Whiteboys, named for the white shirts and frocks they wore to be seen at night, arose in 1761 to "level" the ditches surrounding what had been common land. They destroyed the landlords' grain and flour and invaded houses, looking for guns. They also protested the required tithes to the established church—they were Catholics paying for the upkeep of Protestant clergy. (The Whiteboys didn't want this burden eliminated; they wanted the tithing to be more equitable, says a scholar. This cramped ambition outlines the box they were trapped in.) They also protested the "dues" imposed by their own Catholic priests, posting notices on church doors telling the congregation not to pay. The Catholic poor were in "almost continuous conflict" with their clergy, say historians.

"The Whiteboy association may be considered as a vast trades' union for the protection of the Irish peasantry: the object being, not to regulate the rate of wages, or the hours of work, but to keep the actual occupant in possession of his land," wrote George Cornewall Lewis in the most thorough contemporary account.

The battlelines were not clearly drawn. Most attacks were not against the landlords living in the "Big House," many of whom who were absent or well protected. Instead, it was a guerrilla war of all against all: Farmers fought other farmers; laborers attacked farmers and other laborers. In a fragmented landscape, there were many "middlemen" who leased from landlords, and tenants who sublet land from other tenants. Violence could "spark off in all directions." You knew your station in society, and you fought for it. "Strangers"—anyone outside your county or the few hundred acres of your "townlands" who took a job—could be attacked, their houses "prostrated." The violence was brutal, and it was effective. "Cold fear" held off the tithe collectors and kept many landlords from raising rents, evicting more tenants, and converting more tillage to grazing.

"Every class in this country oppresses the class below it until you come to the most wretched class," one witness told a commission in 1845. "The enemy, at times, in these rural conflicts was the man just above you rather than some shadowy and distant estate owner," says historian

Kevin B. Nowlan. Someone's good fortune was your misfortune. It was a zero-sum life: No one could gain without someone losing.

Ireland's unrest varied greatly from county to county, and within counties among the different estates. Historians are divided over how violent it was in Ireland. However, in a calm period in the mid-1830s, George Lewis observed, "The country is tranquil," but it is the "tranquility of a barrel of gunpowder."

"There is so much permanent misery in the southern and western parts of Ireland," wrote Lewis. "The mass of the country population are in such a state of depression and suffering; they have so little either to hope or to fear, that they are ready at almost any time to break out into disturbances."

These political actions were mixed in with a tradition of petty vengeance and recreational violence that was a school for "rural outrages." Hundreds and sometimes thousands of men fought at fairs, pattern days (patron saint celebrations), funerals, and market days. They belonged to groups—factions—with colorful names: Caravats, Cooleens, Magpies, Peep O'Day Boys, and others. Some of these fights were feuds over old grudges that had gone on so long that they were an inherited habit. Such was the case as the Three Year Olds battled the Four Year Olds over some comment about a calf or colt, no one could remember. Another feud between the Bootashees and Tubbers in County Cork was set off by a fight between two small boys over a game of marbles. That happened around 1794. They were still fighting thirty years later. County Cork was particularly rife with these feuds. There was no neutrality; men were forced to join a "gang."

They fought with enthusiasm, with "heartfelt joy," said a French visitor. Faction fighting was the sport of the countryside. Each man fought with his own special cudgel, a yard long, made from oak, blackthorn, or ash, sometimes cured in the hearth to harden it as a weapon, sometimes with leaded weights. Some men went to battle with two sticks: an eighteen-inch stick to block blows and a four-foot stick for the attack. The men bore many scars—the skull of a Tipperary man was "covered like a chessboard with scars and seams." You never left home without your stick.

Fighting was an expected part of public gatherings. When you were called to a fight, you went. "No matter what was doing, it was left undone," said one County Kerry veteran of twenty-five years of stick fighting. "They'd leave the hay half cut, or the oats to be shelled by the four winds of heaven; and, taking the hay-fork, the reaping-hook, and the scythe in their hands, they'd rush out to massacre each other." In 1827 alone, there were more than one thousand faction fights and riots. The largest fight, the Battle of Ballyeagh, occurred in 1834 as Cooleens and Lawlors faced off, one thousand men on a side, leaving between eighteen to twenty-five dead.

The fights would proceed as if scripted. Before fighting they would "wheel," taunting each other. With the front lines set, one side's leader would strut in front of his men, mocking the other side, impugning the honor and courage of their enemy/neighbor. In reply, their opponents would "wheel," exchanging taunts. At some fights, a leader would trail his coat behind him, making a barnyard-rooster's show, daring the enemy to walk on the "tails of his coat." Sticks and stones, kicking and biting were allowed. Knives were considered cheating, as was piling on. Death was accidental but acceptable (accounting for 41 percent of all homicides in Ireland from 1866 to 1892).

Combatants rarely ended up in court. Even though bystanders might be killed or a pregnant woman might be kicked in the stomach, punishment was light and infrequent. When one witness held up his skull fragments in court, the judge replied, "They would not think anything of that in Clare." Less than 10 percent of homicides by stoning resulted in a jail sentence longer than two years. The authorities, for the most part, stepped aside. In the early nineteenth century, there were failed attempts to form a professional police force and constabulary. Sometimes the militia was called in, and they either stood by or shot into the crowd. The militias compounded the disorder.

The faction fighters fought just to fight, and sometimes they fought for land and against tithes. All this countryside violence was entwined—secret societies with oaths and local grudges fought out over decades, and more spontaneous brawls at fairs and pubs. It was a mix of recreational spite and organized protests. But when the local folks were beating each other up, it may have been hard to classify the fighting. Distinctions were lost in the perpetual melee. Desperate to bring order to the countryside, the Irish and British Parliaments passed a series of acts to "prevent tumultuous risings."

The Irish fighters were observed from the outside—by bishops, by English travelers in Ireland, by Protestant English landlords. Few were sympathetic. They have left us a scrambled record. There was no one, as far as I know, embedded with the Whiteboys, the Heart of Steel, the Pudding Lane Boys, the Shanavests, the Black Hens, no one writing from inside, reporting back in real time. There were recollections and scattered news reports and official commissions, but it's like relying on play-by-play coverage of a football game delivered from outside the stadium. Most of the travelers and officials saw what they were ready to see. The upper classes were content to let the poor destroy each other.

The Corkonians and Far Downs brought this tradition with them. "Provincial spleen" is the dark side of tradition, the darkness beyond the circle of fellowship around the hearth. The fireside could gather neighbors or harden hatred.

When their brawling ways arrived in America, no one understood. They attributed it to religious rancor, but both the Corkonians and the Far Downs were almost all Catholics. They attributed it to whiskey—there were "jigger bosses" on many jobs rationing whiskey throughout the workday—but there was a lot of whiskey and rum about in the country, and it didn't lead to warfare among the laborers. They concluded that it was just the "wild Irish" at it again. "An Irish Fight," was a common headline.

Andrew Leary O'Brien was a rare Irish witness. He had left the seminary and was forced to take a job building the Pennsylvania Canal. The Far Downs and Corkonians "bear a deadly hatred towards each other. . . . One of an opposite party dare not seek employment on a contract where the other party were in employ," said O'Brien, who was from Cork.

> *So deadly was the character of their enmity towards each other, that one of a different party even passing by the other party would be run down like a rabbit by a pack of bloodhounds, & murdered on the spot he was overtaken on.*
>
> *I have seen a number of these men leave their work & run down a man from the next job who was the different party, & beat him with pick and grub hoe handles, till he was so dead that he was not worth another blow.*

There was no relief. They kept a watch over their shanties, "fearing the next party would attack them of nights, & burn & butcher them up while asleep."

The warfare of the Corkonians and Far Downs was not a break in the order. This was the order. The rivals structured the workforce, recruiting workers, reportedly greeting new immigrants dockside. They recruited for the contractors who were hired to build the canals and railroads. The contractors often brought their workers with them from job to job, state to state.

In Ireland, secret societies defended work in their territories; they kept jobs in their families and communities. Each village was a closed shop, closed to "strangers" from just a few miles away. They brought this scarcity outlook with them. Facing dangerous work and employers who disappeared with their pay, there was nothing else for them—no unions, no government regulations or mediators, no laws written to protect workers. There was no place to appeal, no possibility of justice. To these immigrants, America looked like the war of all against all they had left in Ireland. What little they had, they would defend.

They set up national organizations said to be run out of New York City saloons with secret handshakes and passwords. The secret societies were believed to be connected to respectable Irish immigrant aid societies. The Irish-born John Hughes, New York's first Catholic archbishop, threatened that anyone taking an oath to join the societies would be denied last rites: "By taking such oath or obligation, the individual transgresses the laws of God and . . . is necessarily shut out from the privileges of the sacraments and graces of the church."

A map of the Irish riots is a map of public works in North America before the Civil War. A selection of the unrest:

Chesapeake and Ohio Canal, 1834–1840. Ten major riots and strikes introduce the nation to these "Irish fights." The state militia is called in five times, and, for the first time ever, federal troops are deployed against striking workers.

The C&O Canal is always on the verge of financial collapse. In a young country with meager capital, big projects are underfunded. It's an unstable system that promotes conflict. Canals and railroads are built by contractors who bid against keen competition, forcing low bids—there are five hundred bids for the first thirty-four sections of the canal. The contractors hire the labor and run everything; the owners take over only after construction. They pay their contractors monthly, usually withholding 20 percent until the job is finished. It's a cash-starved system. The owners squeeze the contractors, who in turn squeeze their workers. Sometimes they run out of money and don't pay for months. Contractors, realizing that they have underbid, may walk away (in the night), stranding hundreds of unpaid men. They may bring in more workers to drive down wages or, reportedly, instigate fights so some leave and won't have to be paid, says historian Peter Way.

In January 1834, the first major rioting begins after a contractor, whom the company has failed to pay, stops work, dismissing workers without full pay. Hundreds of Corkonians and Far Downs commence a "kind of guerrilla war," attacking each other. Six hundred Far Downs battle three hundred Corkonians. The fighting is "fierce." Five are killed, shot in the head, and many injured. President Andrew Jackson sends in federal troops. A priest gets the warring workers to sign a "treaty of peace."

The treaty, signed by twenty-eight Irish workers before two justices of the peace, is printed in many newspapers:

> *We agree for ourselves, that we will not, either individually or collectively, interrupt or suffer to be interrupted in our presence, any person engaged on the line of the Canal, for or on account of any local difference,*

> *or national prejudice . . . and pledge ourselves in the most solemn manner, to inform on and bring to justice any person, or persons, who may break the pledge contained in this agreement, . . . and we further bind ourselves to the State of Maryland, each in the sum of twenty dollars—to keep the peace towards each other, as well as towards the citizens of the State.*

But the battles continue: March 1834, three dead. June 1834, three dead, beat up German workers to drive them off the job. February 1835, a fifteen-day strike until troops force them back to work. February 1836, fighting resumes between the Corkonians and the Far Downs; remaining German workers are driven off. Spring 1836, Dutch workers driven from the job. Spring 1837, forty English miners brought in to dig a tunnel are attacked; a year later, only two remain. January 1838, four hundred canal workers, unpaid for a month, ransack a nearby town. Months later, still without pay, some are starving. The company offers fifty cents on the dollar. The workers refuse, demanding "all or none." They threaten to wreck the canal, seizing 140 kegs of gunpowder to blow up the locks. The militia is called again, but they refuse at first because they're owed for the last call-up. Finally, they get the workers to surrender the gunpowder without a fight. The company pays the back wages. Work and rioting resume for years.

Baltimore and Ohio Railroad, 1834. The B&O, built to compete with the C&O, is its twin in nationally reported violence. June 1834, Corkonians and Far Downs, each with four to five hundred men, battle with pikes, bludgeons, and maybe firearms. They burn down each other's shanties. At least four are killed, including a woman. One Baltimore newspaper calls it "The War." November 1834, eight to ten workers severely beat two contractors. In another assault, they kill a contractor and his assistant. Troops arrive and arrest three hundred workers. No one will talk. Workers who refuse to join the rioting are beaten and sometimes killed in midnight raids.

Winter 1850, there's serious violence when the chief engineer, Benjamin Henry Latrobe Jr., brings in 2,500 immigrants from New York City. They are attacked. "The hands here are disposed to be turbulent," says Latrobe. March 1851, in a "murderous assault" on six or eight men sleeping in a shanty, twenty-five men try to burn it down. Failing that, they tell the men inside they will "relent." The men surrender and are beaten in a "most brutal and savage manner."

Boston and Providence Railroad, April 1834. One hundred men armed with clubs and stones hunt down and beat up two contractors. Another hundred join them and shut down all work.

Baltimore and Washington Railroad, June 1834. "A furious insurrection."

Wabash and Erie Canal, Indiana, July 1835. Work stops when six hundred Corkonians and Far Downs, separated by fifty miles, march to battle on a date and at a site both have chosen. To arm themselves, the canal workers rob houses, threatening to murder residents. They hold up a wagon to steal three kegs of gunpowder. The Corkonians steal a cannon, setting it on the battlefield in a "strong military position," but lacking shot, they load it with gravel. A canal commissioner intervenes to negotiate a truce, which the militia uses to arrest hundreds; others flee. Most of the men are released to return to work. The "Indiana Irish Wars" continue and spread to the Madison and Indiana Railroad in August 1837.

Illinois and Michigan Canal, June 1838. A wage cut sparks a widespread "Irish War."

New York and Hudson River Railroad, June 1839. "Tremendous fight. . . . Ringleaders escape."

Croton Water Works, New York, May 1841. Corkonians and Far Downs fight for two hours, leaving one dead and many "laid up with broken heads, bruises, etc." There are frequent nightly "disturbances" and "all kinds of outrages." Stables and other buildings are torched. Three hundred workers swarm a contractor's house, tearing it down. One boss is "beaten nearly to death" with clubs and stones by three men he has fired.

Western Railroad, Massachusetts, July 1841. The Springfield militia arrive after a "bloody contest" between the Corkonians and Far Downs. "No lives have been lost, thus far."

"Welland Canal War," Ontario, July, September, and November 1842. "Bands of dangerous men, armed, are prowling about in all directions," entering the houses in St. Catherines. "The District is in a state of anarchy." One hundred fifty armed volunteers stand watch. "Hordes of Irish Laborers . . . have been pouring into this village," but there's only employment for one-tenth of them. About 1,300 men and women are camped out near town, without work or food. By January 1835, there are ten thousand hungry men, women, and children. The Corkonians and Far Downs battle each other to get whatever work there is, overrunning St. Catherines as they chase their enemies, sending them "flying in all directions through houses, yards, and over fences." Two priests try to keep the warring parties apart. British troops and militia arrest men from both sides, filling the jail—where they continue their brawl.

Lachine Canal, near Montreal, January to March 1843. More than 1,100 workers strike for higher wages after their pay was cut by a third. Rival gangs march in intimidating torchlight parades, sometimes through Montreal. Corkonians raid and destroy the shanties of Far Downs, attacking with heavy gunfire.

New York and Erie Railroad, December 1847. Far Downs try to remove the Corkonians and Dutch workers from the job. In midnight raids, they "traversed the whole line, compelling the proscribed laborers to quit work, beating and abusing them with much severity," killing one worker. Defending themselves, the Dutch form two platoons and open fire, holding off the Far Downs and taking two as prisoners.

Lowell, Massachusetts, September 1849. "A serious riot." Many wounded, including a boy who was shot. Police and firemen disperse the two sides.

Blue Ridge Railroad, Virginia, January 1850. Corkonians with pistols and cudgels chase Far Downs out of their shanties. The militia arrests sixty men.

Central Railroad, near Pittsburgh, September 1850. "Another railroad riot. . . . Disgraceful."

Steubenville and Indiana Railroad, January 1852. The Corkonians storm "Section Four" to demolish the Far Downs' shanties. The next day, in the city, the Far Downs intercept some Corkonians, attacking with "guns and clubs." Word reaches the Corkonians on Section Four, who organize to march to the city. Steubenville rises to defend itself—fire alarms ring, citizens take arms, the mayor, sheriff and the militia prepare for battle. "A large cannon, loaded to the muzzle with paving stones," defends the main road. The Corkonians, "seeing what preparations had been made for them," retreat. The Far Downs are trapped in the city. They are "out of work and out of money. The Corkonians keeping possession of Section Four."

Hostilities continue the next month: Four hundred Far Downs raid the Corkonian shanties and "indiscriminately fired upon men, women and children." They ransack the shanties and set them on fire. "A posse of armed men," the Steubenville City Greys, assisted by twenty farmers, round up most of the Far Downs, but fifty-seven elude them for another assault and kill a Corkonian, shooting him in the "main artery of the thigh" before bludgeoning him to death. Another group of Far Downs invades farmhouses, searching for Corkonians. All work on the line is suspended. In response, two to three hundred Corkonians, armed with shotguns and muskets, abandon the railroad they are building near Pittsburgh to go aid their allies forty miles away in Steubenville, but the steamboat captains refuse to take them.

Buffalo and State Line Railroad, September 1852. Two hundred Corkonians from one work section, "mostly armed with guns, axes, shovels, picks, pick handles, pitch-forks, and clubs," march to another section to "drive off" their rivals, destroying their shanties. They have fought before.

Erie Railroad, Hudson City, New Jersey, March 1857. Five hundred Irish riot from the early afternoon through the night . . .

Rioting was common. "In all, there were ninety-one riots on American and Canadian canals in the thirty-year period beginning in 1820, the vast majority of which involved faction fights," says historian Peter Way.

"The Great Riot Year" of 1834 began with the C&O Canal riots and ended with the Irish rioting on the B&O Railroad in November. In between, there were many riots that weren't started by the Irish. There was a race riot (Philadelphia), Election Day riots (Philadelphia and New York City), a bank riot (Portsmouth, New Hampshire), anti-Mormon riots (Missouri), anti-abolitionist riots (all over), and anti-Catholic riots (all over). The anti-Catholic riots were waged against Irish immigrants.

The following year saw more race riots (Washington, Philadelphia, St. Louis, and Georgia), another bank riot (Baltimore), a riot between competing fire departments (Baltimore), a German labor riot (Baltimore and Washington Railroad), a mob lynching of five gamblers (Vicksburg, Mississippi), a Catholic mob attacking a Protestant anti-Catholic meeting (New York), and more anti-abolitionist riots (all over).

Most Americans, of course, only read about the rioting, but it was like a traveling circus that might come to your town. In the late 1840s, the Cheshire Railroad brought the show to a striving mill town in New Hampshire. The 1848 riot near Keene was just another chapter in the war between the Corkonians and Far Downs, and it may have been fought by men who had battled at other canals and railroads.

II. "There Is No Better-Built Railroad in the Country."

The railroad was everything in nineteenth-century America—the promise of prosperity, the promise of "iron bands" to bind the distant states of the young union. Railroads "annihilated space and time"; they nullified distance. The grinding slowness of getting anywhere—days of travel by horse or oxen, days under sail or on a narrow canal boat—would be overturned. Mountains and rivers would no longer be obstacles. Railroads would bring order to a disorderly nation; they would ensure that the American experiment in self-government survived. Americans believed in railroads; they built them everywhere, pushing up steeper hills and twisting around tighter turns than in Europe. They urged engineers to run their steam locomotives fast, risking accidents. In just fifteen years America would build the largest network of railroads in the world. "The old nations of the earth creep on at a snail's pace," said the industrialist Andrew Carnegie. "The Republic thunders past with the rush of the express."

No one wanted to be left out. Every spot on the map competed for a railroad. States subsidized them, granting land and financing bonds; civic leaders organized investors to entice a railroad to come their way. Having a railroad line or two could be the making of your town, city, business, or farm. It's why some villages laid out wide boulevards that were only muddy ways between trees, fields, and a few scattered houses.

Keene was like the rest, a big mill town with 2,610 people in 1840 set on flat land in the corner of New Hampshire, sixteen miles from the Connecticut River and Vermont. Keene was proud of its wide Main Street—just two years after the first White settlers founded the town, they doubled the width of the street, and when it was paved with concrete in 1921, the chamber of commerce boasted that it was the "widest paved Main Street in the world."

Keene's leading businessmen petitioned the state legislature to charter a railroad in 1835. It would take ten years to find investors, adjust the route, petition the legislature again, and begin construction. The Cheshire Railroad would run nearly fifty-four miles northwest from a town south of the state line in Ashburnham, Massachusetts, through Keene, and up to Bellows Falls in Vermont, another mill town awaiting a railroad.

The railroad hired two of the nation's leading civil engineers to plan the route and design twenty granite arch bridges. The largest bridge "ranks among the most impressive masonry arches built in the United States before 1850," say railroad historians Bradford G. Blodget and Richard R. Richards Jr. "The Cheshire was engineered to a gold standard and built to last a millennium. It was widely hailed as one of the great engineering feats in New England."

"We have seldom passed over a road constructed as well," said *The American Railroad Journal.* A correspondent for *The Mining Journal* concurred, "There is no better built railroad in the country, than that part of the Cheshire which is now completed. . . . We cannot fail to rejoice in it, as a triumph of human skill and enterprise, great as any that valor wins."

The first train from Boston arrived in Keene on May 16, 1848, at 1:30 p.m., where five thousand waited, far greater than the town's population. This was the first train many had seen. Shops were closed; the town was celebrating a holiday. Cannons south of the city announced the approaching train—two new locomotives pulling fifteen cars decorated with flags and evergreen boughs. Boston's mayor was aboard, along with railroad officials, investors, and a Boston brass band. As the train arrived, more cannons fired, church bells rang, and the big crowd cheered in a way we only see at big games when there's a home run or a touchdown, but they were cheering progress. It wasn't a concept—it was a railroad. Great things were imminent. Already, in the years when track was being laid miles from town, there was a building boom in Keene.

Today in a bank at the head of the square, a large mural celebrates Keene's first train. There's a lot of blue sky in the mural, women in elegant hoop skirts and holding parasols, and men with top hats and frock coats. It looks like they are getting ready for a formal ballroom dance. A small gray cloud rises from the locomotive as it comes to a stop. This was more than Boston coming to a New Hampshire town—Keene had joined to the world. Once the Cheshire Railroad was complete, passengers and freight could travel over railroads from Boston to Montreal.

But ahead was an obstacle. Leaving Keene, which sat on a glacial lakebed, the railroad had to rise 830 feet, a challenging climb. Most of what blocked the way was granite. The railroad's engineer considered his options. The railroad would have to cut down through forty feet of granite (about four stories) for more than half a mile (three thousand feet). This cut would yield a desired grade of sixty feet per mile leaving Keene. A "lesser cut" would require a locomotive to pull a train up an incline of seventy-five feet every mile, until it reached the summit in Surry. Downhill, off the summit, also could be a steep seventy-five feet a mile. The engineer was still working out the route and "had some reason to believe" he could find a line that would descend more modestly, at sixty feet per mile, he reported.

The editor of the *Vermont Phoenix* in Brattleboro received the engineer's report with skepticism. "These, as our readers will perceive, are much steeper grades than can be found in New England, except upon the Western [Massachusetts] railroad, which is almost the only unprofitable road in New England. If the friends of the Keene route can gather consolation from such facts, they are easily consoled."

The engineer did find a more modest route and lessened the incline by blasting even deeper into the summit, fifty feet deep in places. As built, the maximum grade was just shy of sixty feet for six miles approaching the summit and eight miles after. But the newspaper editor was right about the cost.

Making the Summit Cut, along with the high construction standards on the entire line, had put the Cheshire Railroad in debt. By 1850 they had spent $2.6 million on construction and interest on loans, or $107 million in today's dollars—almost $2 million a mile (at a time when the US economy was much smaller than it is today, more than seventeen thousand times smaller). About 10 percent of the expenses were just for masonry, the stone arch bridges, and about a dozen granite culverts. Adding to the debt were a roadbed wide enough to add a parallel track, the heaviest weight iron rails in use, a large locomotive repair shop, turntables and roundhouses, nine railroad stations, wooden bridges, and the required fences to enclose most of the fifty-four-mile route.

"With regard to our indebtedness, it may be remarked that it has been well known that the cost of the road has very considerably exceeded the amount of means provided by the stockholders," said the railroad's 1850 annual report. "This result has been so familiar from its general occurrence in railroad enterprises, that, however inconvenient it may be, and however much to be regretted, it has almost ceased to excite anything like surprise." The railroad's directors would go back to the original stockholders ten times for more money.

The summit delayed the opening of the northern part of the route for three years. The challenge reportedly ruined several contractors who gave up, but only one contractor is on record. He had to master New Hampshire's stubborn granite and his workers, the Corkonians and the Far Downs.

The contractor, Captain Edward E. Parmele, employed more than two hundred Irishmen at the summit by the second year of construction in 1848. They lived in a shanty village. The Corkonians and Far Downs were segregated by some unknown distance or divider. The married men lived in shanties that were twenty-five feet long by fifteen feet wide; unmarried men bunked in larger dormitory shanties. There were sixty school-age children in the village taught by two teachers hired by the

Ladies Charitable Society in Keene; Miss Soule taught for ten weeks in spring and summer, and Miss Nancy Towns taught the fall term in a new shanty the society had built for a classroom. At Keene's annual town meeting in 1848, Deacon Stewart Hastings petitioned the town to support the school. They obliged, allocating $50—about $2,000 today—from the "literary fund."

Nothing has come down to us about the living conditions in the village, even though people from Keene visited to have a look at the "Irish village." With stables for the work horses and oxen, sheds for the tools and derricks, and a company store, the Irish village was, for its time, a small metropolis. Its foreign-born population—between three and four hundred—was about two-thirds of the size of the town it inhabited. Surry had about five hundred people (its peak before a century-long decline). The Ladies Charitable Society visited, but at least in their minutes, they were too much the proper ladies to comment on what they saw. The society was run by the wives of the three leading clergymen in town; they saw much, heard much, and said nothing. They prized discretion, as they sought to do "good works" quietly.

One newspaper notice about an "unfortunate accident" hinted at their presence at the summit: "A very promising boy, eight years old, of one of the Irish laborers, was playing on a pile of heavy stones, which had been deposited on a declivity near the shanty, when the stone he was on, weighing several hundreds, tipped and threw the youth in the same direction, and he was crushed to death in an instant."

Promising is a word teachers may use. This is the only kind word the *Sentinel* published about the Irish workers.

The Irish workers had to move a mountain by hand. They started on the rock, drilling into it with one man, called the shaker, holding a metal shaft with a sharpened steel bit, as another man hit it with a heavy sledgehammer, over and over. After each hit, the shaker would turn the bit and change it when it became dull. The team would switch positions. This was known as double jacking. To speed things up, two men would take alternating swings at the bit. (If they were out of sync, they'd slow down the drilling.) Teams of men were spread out over the ridge, plinking away, an impossible mismatch. With a drill bit one inch in diameter, it could take an hour to advance one inch. Once they had drilled a hole, they would fill it with gunpowder and a fuse, which also had gunpowder. The fuse would be lit, the men would scatter, and chunks of the stone would heave upward and come crashing down. Gunpowder was volatile—a spark from metal hitting rock as the powder was pounded down or even from static electricity could set it off. Dynamite was more stable and more powerful, but it was not yet invented. Many workmen were killed by explosions.

In the second year of work, the contractor, Parmele, brought in three steam-powered drills, an innovation. This is a very early use of this technology. There is only one powered drill on record. Known as a drop drill, it would lift a drilling bar and let it drop, lift and let it drop. Gravity was the driving force. It's not known how effective this was, but it must have been better than pounding rock by hand. A reliable, percussive, steam-powered drill wouldn't be in use for another twenty years.

They would drill down, blast, and cart off the stone to be cut into large blocks for walls, granite drains, and culverts, or smashed by men swinging sledgehammers to make ballast for the railbed. Hundreds of men would have been hoisting stones with derricks, loading them on ox and horse carts, unloading stone, hammering the stone to shape, and hoisting it again to where it was needed to build large retaining walls to hold back the hillside. The drill would be reset on a new, lower level and powered up by its steam engine to repeat the forceful drive downward. One day's work, in good weather or bad, in rain or snow, was like all the other days. The Summit Cut was essentially a granite quarry more than a half-mile long, and it was just one of three deep cuts the railroad had to make to escape the valley. Nearing the end, pushing on with "all vigor," the contractors put their men to work at night (illuminated just how—with large torches?). They had eleven thousand cubic yards of rock left to remove—about one hundred thousand wheelbarrow loads.

If you visit the Summit Cut today, you can still see the neat, cylindrical lines left by the steam-powered drill, holes that were three inches in diameter, to be filled with gunpowder. The lines are as trim as pleats in a skirt. Some of these lines are memorials that are invisible to us, places where men were blown up, or crushed by a stone slipping from a ledge or a derrick. They mark a moment when work paused, the dead or injured were carted off, the contractor inspected the site, and work immediately resumed. At this spot, a man from County Cork was killed; at this spot, a man from County Longford was maimed; at this spot, a man's body had to be gathered up, piece by piece, from among the exploded rocks. This is the hidden history of the granite ledge, split forever for a clean line from Keene to Bellows Falls.

None of this work made the newspapers, except for the arrival of the steam-powered drills. This great earthwork was invisible. It was as if a teeming workforce was raising a pyramid on your town's common, and no one said a word. The Irish were only news when they were rioting, as they did in 1848, in the first story I had read. But as I dug deeper, I learned that there had been other riots at the summit.

In June 1847, the Irish at the summit erupted in rioting. "Our peaceful village was made the scene of no small excitement," reported the *Keene Philanthropist*. "On Sunday riotous proceedings were had among the workmen, by whom assaults were made upon one another. Eyes were blackened, faces bruised and other outrages committed." That evening, Parmele was called, but he was halted on the road by the rioters and couldn't reach the "scene of carnage."

The next day, Parmele sent the constable "to arrest the ring leaders." The constable corralled two or three of them, but the workers freed his prisoners. He rode back to Keene to get "Capt. Gerould of the Keene Lights, who immediately called out some fifty men, who, with guns and bayonets, repaired to the spot. . . . The rioters fled into the woods, but were pursued and three were arrested." Part of the Keene Light Infantry remained at the Summit Cut overnight and returned Tuesday morning with five more rioters, including the wife of one rioter. The "worst ones" had evaded arrest, said the *New Hampshire Sentinel*.

"The sole cause of the riot and disturbance in this case, as in almost every other difficulty on the line, was *rum, rum*," said the *Sentinel*'s story

"Rum and Riot." "We learn that the men had been paid off on Saturday, and that about ten o'clock at night, *three barrels* of rum were sent up there from the Railroad Store in this town. . . . The consequence was what might have been expected—a drunken quarrel the next day." For more than a year, "rum has been sold in immense quantities along the line of road." This was "not only disgraceful to our village" and a "moral evil," but it also was endangering the contractor and delaying the opening of the railroad.

Parmele, the "energetic contractor," put Keene on notice that the rum sales had to stop. He confiscated the remaining barrels of rum he found in the shanty village and had them returned to Keene. His men dumped the barrels on the town common, where the barrel "heads were afterwards knocked in and contents spilled upon the ground. All effort to set fire to this liquor failed," said the *Sentinel.* "We are informed that it was a vile compound of rum, water and India cockle, calculated to make men crazy and drunk at a very small cost to the traders engaged in this vile business." Parmele also had two out-of-town men arrested for "selling spiritous liquors" at the summit.

Almost every story about the Irish riots on canals and railroads blames drinking. To many observers, it was the cause; to others, it was the accelerant to unseen grievances. Many Americans thought that whiskey was the alpha and omega of the Irish immigrants' lives.

The Irish found themselves on the wrong side of a growing temperance movement. Drinking in the United States surged from 1790 into the 1830s, when Americans consumed nearly three times the amount they do today, says historian W. J. Rorabaugh. They drank more than the Irish or the English, until drinking "quite suddenly leveled off" and "began to plummet toward an unprecedented low." At the country's founding, alcohol was a "good creature" thought to be nutritious. Rum, whiskey, and hard cider relieved a monotonous diet of corn and salt pork and in some cities replaced unsafe drinking water. The temperance crusaders recast alcohol as an evil with the villainous name of "demon rum." Starting in the 1810s, ministers began a temperance movement that would span the century and lead, after great effort, to the Eighteenth Amendment to the Constitution in 1919, establishing Prohibition.

By the 1840s, when the men were blasting through the summit, drinking had slowed in the middle and professional classes, but it was robust on the frontier and among river boatmen, lumberjacks, stage drivers, canal builders, and other hard laborers. Some canal diggers were given as much as a pint of rum a day to keep digging. Outside the workers' camps, alcohol was evil, a moral failing, a sin. In the camps and shanty villages, after ten or twelve hours of hard labor and injuries both minor and serious, a drink of rum or whiskey was relief and recreation. Blaming a riot on rum excused the public from inquiring about working conditions, wages, unfair bosses, the hardship of being so far from home, and the imported disputes that set Irishmen against one another.

The riot the next year, in 1848, was far worse. A fight "had been brewing for some time" between the Corkonians and the Far Downs as they worked on adjoining sections, said the *Sentinel*, which wrongly identified the Corkonian's opponents as "Limericks." This is a mistake. County Limerick borders Cork. The newspaper probably confused either County Leitrim or Leinster, a province of the Far Downs. Such carelessness was another sign of contempt for the immigrants. "So desperate had the parties become that the Keene stages did not pass over their regular route for two days," reported the *Boston Evening Transcript*. A "kind of rum fight" had begun on Sunday night, said Parmele, and continued past dawn.

At noon on Monday, August 21, some two hundred Corkonians assembled to attack the shanties of the Far Downs. The Far Downs were outnumbered—no count is given—and only "partially prepared." The warring parties met just two hundred feet apart, with Parmele standing between them, trying to prevent the battle. This is the most intriguing detail, a hint that they were reenacting the faction fights of Ireland, with one side "wheeling," taunting the other, and the contractor playing the role of the parish priest trying to keep the peace. It's only a hint, but the entire battle matches the description of every Irish faction brawl, except that in America both sides were armed.

At close range, they opened fire. One man was killed, and two were "badly wounded" by the "repeated volleys." "Some others had balls through their clothes, and the lives of many were much in peril, including that of Capt. Parmele, the contractor, who was for some time between the fire of the parties, trying to stop the affray," said the *Sentinel.* The dead man was Michael Tracy, reportedly from Cork. He was named in only one local paper, the *Cheshire Republican and Farmer*.

The Corkonians overran the Far Downs and swarmed through their shanties, smashing "stoves, tables, looking-glasses, furniture, trunks" and stealing cash. The mayhem continued for three hours. Once again, the Keene Light Infantry was called, late, arriving to find that most of the rioters had fled to the woods, where they continued firing at the shanties and throwing cobblestones at the militia. The Keene Lights, joined by the Westmoreland Lights, stayed the night. In the morning, they marched into the woods, the men "20 rods apart" (110 yards), with orders to shoot only if the "enemy showed fight." They arrested about forty men. The riot made the news around the country and overseas, being reported in Boston, New York City, Buffalo, Baltimore, Washington, New Orleans, Louisville, and London. "A Real Irish Battle," said one headline; "Desperate Railroad Riot," said other headlines.

"The feud is of such a character that the two parties cannot again work in the vicinity of each other. The Corkonians must be driven out of the state or captured," said the *Sentinel* in its only story on the riot. "It will be . . . a cause of rejoicing when we are freed of this quarrelsome and rummy population." It was just more "rum and riot" to the *Sentinel*'s editors. But the riot's cause could be found in their own newspaper, two weeks later, on September 5: "The great rock cut on the summit section is all finished, and the roadbed is now being prepared."

The Summit Cut was open; tracks were being laid. Far fewer workers were needed. The Corkonians were trying to remove the Far Downs so they could have the remaining jobs. They had done this all over the country, on the C&O Canal, the B&O Railroad, the Wabash and Erie Canal, and many others—really any place they worked. This was standard operating practice in Ireland, where various secret societies fought to control the work digging one of the earliest canals, the Royal Canal.

A month later, on October 19, Parmele and his partner, H. C. Ward, advertised,

AUCTION!
GREAT SALE OF RAILROAD PROPERTY!

> HORSES; HARNESSES; ONE AND TWO HORSE WAGONS; HORSE AND OX CARTS; CARS; DERRICKS; PICKS; SHOVELS; CROWBARS; CHAINS; DRILLS; HAMMERS; HOUSEHOLD FURNITURE; STORE GOODS AND FIXTURES; SHANTIES AND OTHER BUILDINGS; AND VARIOUS OTHER ARTICLES—TOO NUMEROUS TO MENTION.

Their work was done. They were getting out of town.

"On Monday a whole herd of Irishmen were tried for being engaged in a riot," reported the *Republican and Farmer* on September 21, 1848. Twenty-one of the rioters were brought into the Cheshire Court of Common Pleas in the case of the *State v. Murphy, et al.*, to be heard before a jury. Some of the men had been sitting in jail for weeks. Bail had been set at a steep rate, ranging from $75 to $150 (about $3,000 to $6,000 today). Initially only four workers could post that amount. Railroad construction usually paid between a dollar and a dollar and a half a day (forty to sixty dollars). Their case was heard at the end of September, a month after the riot. (The lead defendant, Michael Murphy, didn't show up in court.)

They were charged with "unlawfully riotously" assembling "to disturb the peace of this state . . . with diverse dangerous and deadly weapons towit, with guns, clubs, and stones, and other dangerous and offensive weapons," to "attack and beset the dwelling houses in the possession of one Patrick Caton and one Michael Wards" for "three hours to the great fear and terror of the people and the said dwelling houses . . . and did break and demolish the furniture of the said Caton and the said Wards."

Caton and Wards were probably their bosses. No aggrieved Far Downs are named; they would have never talked in court. It would have been worth their lives. There is no mention of any dead or wounded men. Further, the charge read, the rioters "being in said dwelling houses and did then and there fire and discharge loaded guns and hurl stones in and among certain peaceable citizens of this state"—five men who were probably in the Keene or Westmoreland Lights.

The defendants, the "herd of Irishmen," were named:

> *Michael Murphy, Jerry Cockley, Timothy Crowley, John Conners, Decklin Conklin, Laurence Crowley, John Conner, Dennis Sullivan 1st, Timothy Driscoll, Daniel Delany, Martin Cunningham, John Flatherly, William O'Donnell, John Tracy, James Donovan, Dennis Collins, Thomas Brotherick, Edward Delany, Dennis Sullivan 4th, James Fitzpatrick, and Dennis Crowley, together with other evil disposed persons whose names are unknown to the jurors to the number of 200.*

Murphy, Cockley, Crowley, etc. These are Cork and possibly Kerry names. No Far Downs.

The names are the most astonishing part of the record. It's as if these men had stepped out of the nameless nowhere of stone and mud, rum and rumor, to take shape. We know the names of the civil engineers who laid out the Cheshire Railroad. We know the names of the railroad's board of directors. But the Irish workers get names only here. In court the Irishmen appear, are named, tried, and disappear.

They all pled not guilty, and the judge gave the case to the jury. "After being out a short time the jury returned a verdict of guilty" against seventeen of the twenty-one men. "In consideration that those found guilty were not the ringleaders in the riot, the court fined them only $30 each and costs [$12], and very properly administered to them some wholesome words of advice to their future obedience to the laws, and leading quiet lives under the common protection of those laws," said the *Republican and Farmer.*

Michael Murphy and company were ordered to pay forty-two dollars. And then what? Did they pay? Were they jailed until they paid? We don't know. There are no more court records, no more press reports. The Irish were released to invisibility and contempt.

Writing almost fifty years later, one member of the Keene Light Infantry recalled that they had been called out a "dozen times or more before the road was completed."

III. The Buried Past

The Irish left, the Cheshire Railroad opened and operated for forty-five years before it merged with a larger railroad, which was then taken over by the largest railroad in New England, the Boston and Maine. Captain Parmele went to work as a contractor to build part of the Buffalo and Lockport Railroad in New York, and later railroads in Missouri, Iowa, Mississippi, Louisiana, and sections of the great transcontinental Union Pacific Railroad. The shanties of the Irish village were sold at auction, and the village disappeared many times over. No one knows where it was, but from studying old maps and the clues offered by the reports of the riots, I believe that the site of the Irish village is buried under 850,000 tons of trash. Keene's Transfer Station, its dump, sits right by the Cheshire's railbed. A tall, grass-covered dome rises steeply, covering twenty acres.

In the 1840s the Summit Road ran here close to the railroad. Supplies would have come up this road from Keene. This is the road where Parmele was stopped during the 1847 riot, and it's the road that the Keene Stages couldn't use during the 1848 riot. The dump sits just before the big Summit Cut. It's the logical staging ground. The Summit Road, now Route 12, was moved uphill in 1948—through a new rock cut—and today takes a big bend around the dump. A stub of the old Summit Road remains; it's the entrance road and address for Keene's dump. The town line for Surry crosses in front of the dump's gate.

The land near and under Route 12 is the other likely site for the village. It's possible that the Corkonians were housed on one side of the railroad, uphill just before the Surry town line, and the Far Downs were downhill, across the tracks and the road, down just a ways, where the trash mountain is today. They would have wanted as much of a barrier as they could find to keep apart the Corkonians and Far Downs. (During the day, they worked with their own crews, on different sections.) A railroad running through a granite trench was a pretty good barrier but apparently not good enough. Either way, under the trash or under the road, the site of what may be the largest labor battle in northern New England's history has vanished. The Irish history is lost—except for the workers who were left behind.

The history of Surry, published in 1922, says that there are "thirty or more" Irish workers buried "without stones" in the town's Southwest Burying Yard.

I put a small Post-It Note in my wallet:

S. E. Part of Yard
4 rods square
30+ Irish

And I went to look for the Irish.

The Burying Yard is off by itself at the end of a dirt road and not easy to find. I ran into two dead ends—two dirt roads that ran out into Class 6 trails, one road ending in a rutted, washed-out, steep path. Squinting at my topographical map, I saw for the first time that the road became a dotted line.

One of those closed roads ran uphill from the Summit Cut. This was the nearest graveyard. Even in its day, the yard was off by itself, with its closest neighbor, the town's poor farm. The poor and the dead, ye shall always have with you. Today, it's still off by itself, except for a new house across the road whose inhabitants eyed me warily.

The yard is a quiet ground; old stone walls, moss, ferns, tall headstones. The last burial was 120 years ago. The Irish were deposited and forgotten. Standing there, I felt that these Irishmen needed a memorial, but not a historical marker or a mourning and a keening. They needed music and poetry. I don't know why I thought this, but in the lonesome burying ground, it was as clear as a written request. There, among the neglected Irish, the idea found me.

Many months later, I came across the Irish word for such a gathering: a *ceili* (pronounced *kay-lee*). These men, and possibly women and children, from Cork and the north would welcome a ceili. I resolved to return with a ceili, a small one but enough music and poetry to break the fast, to break 180 years of silence.

A ceili is a visit, and more than that, it's a way of "passing the time," says folklorist Henry Glassie.

> *People enter without invitation or forewarning. The company grows, diminishes, shifts through the evening with a minimum of ceremony to mark changes or disrupt the chat circling the hearth. Greetings are brief and made on the move, people join conversations raised before their arrival and leave without waiting for resolution. Like the fire, like the world, the chat was going on before their coming, will be going after their leaving. Life, they say, is just a little ceili. The ceili is just a little life. . . . Another night, and they will be together again with the same topics to discuss. Nothing starts or stops, exactly. Things go on.*

The ceili is the community gathered around the hearth. Life and fire. We'd bring a little warmth to that cold stone burial ground.

I recruited my ceili, asking two friends, Steve Schuch and Henry Walters, one a musician and the other a poet. Steve, with his Night Heron Consort, plays deeply felt Celtic music. Steve had won fiddling championships and arts fellowships, but mostly what I knew about his music was from when we'd perform alongside each other on evenings that mixed poetry with his violin, guitar, and singing. Steve conquers a room with the first few notes on his violin or guitar. The entire room leans toward him, relaxes, and is ready to go wherever he'll take them.

Like Steve, Henry is a spellbinder. Henry is a poet, with his first two books and poems in leading literary journals, a master falconer with a growing business teaching falconry, and basically a wizard with anything he does, whether it's playing Chopin, translating other poets, acting with a local theater company, designing and building his own cabin, or just baking bread. His travels had brought him to study falconry in Ireland for two years and beekeeping in a family's olive grove in Sicily for a year. To both Steve and Henry, there was nothing strange about heading out to enliven an old graveyard. When I'd asked them, their only question was, "When?"

Steve and I drove together to meet Henry in the Home Depot parking lot in Keene. He was meeting Steve for the first time. Steve immediately lobbied for libations, for bringing some Guinness with us. I thought this was a bad idea. Three guys standing around in an old cemetery, drinking beer, isn't a good look. I explained how suspicious the people across the road were. They called out, "What are you doing? Are you taking pictures of my house?" The end of their driveway is watched over by no fewer than three motion-detecting cameras and a sign—a metal, highway-department-grade sign—warning you not to turn around in their driveway. My caution was turned aside. I was overruled. Henry was all for it. He dashed into the Price Chopper to buy beer. When he came trotting out with the beer under one arm, looking as if he'd just pulled off a small heist, it felt like we were three high school kids sneaking off to drink beer in the woods, to "skip some school; act real cool."

We drove out of Keene. The paved-parking-lot world falls away fast. We followed the old Third New Hampshire Turnpike. Don't be deceived—it's a two-lane backcountry route that was chartered in 1799. We turned off where a dirt road rose past a dairy farm and entered the trees. At the dead end, we got out. We were by ourselves on a damp, chilly, overcast April afternoon. The unfriendly neighbors were not home. I hadn't told Steve and Henry what to expect in the Southwest Burying Yard. I wanted them to be as surprised as I was on my first visit.

The southeast corner, said to be four rods by four rods (sixty-six feet by sixty-six feet), was listed as having unmarked graves, "thirty or more." But they are marked by stones. No carved headstones, no inscriptions, just the ancient stones picked up on-site and planted with the dead.

The small scatter of stones in irregular lines, like a retreating army, is a sad sight, a thwarted commemoration. The soft ground is slumped and uneven. It was wild beyond its small confines.

I had counted maybe twenty stones on my first visit, but I got a different count each time. The corner closest to the road was thick with spongy moss, which must have covered other stones. In spots it was up for debate if a stone was a monument or just part of the usual ridge-backed New Hampshire land.

"Moss," said the English moralist John Ruskin, is the "first mercy of the earth, veiling with hushed softness its dintless rocks." Underfoot, I could feel submerged stones like a bony back. One stone stands taller, a slender granite shard, an exclamation point rising like a boundary marker. Why? Was this a tribute to a great man, a beloved brother? Or was it just a boundary marker? We'll never know.

I had paced it off, coming up with a depth of about fifty feet, not four rods—sixty-six feet—but the other measure ran true. The Irish section stretched to a large pine-tree stump. The pine had recently shaded the yard. The rings showed it had lived about 110 years. The tree stump was a clock marking the centuries. The pine had started growing around 1890; it was cut down in 2010. This tree had lived more than a century before it died, and that still didn't cover the time since these Irish workers had been buried here. They have been gone that long.

Uphill in the rest of the yard, away from the Catholic Irish, were the Protestant Yankees, buried under tall headstones facing away from the Irish, facing uphill to the west, as was common practice—sixty-seven in all, interred from 1800 to 1906, awaiting the Resurrection and Last Judgment.

Steve and Henry surveyed the scene, a graveyard unlike any they had ever seen.

"The graveyard is partitioned by moss," Henry said. The rest of the yard with the thin, black slate stones, so upright they seem like they are judging you, stand on the grass. Sphagnum moss thrives where it is wet. This is a wet corner—too wet for burial until the town of Surry sold or gave it to the railroad. The old Yankees wouldn't bury their families here—give it to the Irish.

By late summer, the Irish corner is a field of ferns, a small, light green forest of these ancient plants, shimmering, waving, making unseen stirrings visible. The stones disappear. Covered with ferns or just the green carpet of moss, the Irish section seems like an ancient Celtic landscape, with the deep silence of neolithic stones that you come across everywhere—circles, lines, lone standing stones, mysteries all.

Henry leaned down and parted the moss from the base of one stone that was about six inches tall. He wanted more—a name, a word, something to stand against oblivion.

"It's as if you're watching the act of forgetting, because they're stones," I said. "They're not headstones. They're not carved. They're just pulled from stone walls, from the earth, and people walk away," I said.

"You say the act of forgetting?" Steve asked.

"That's the way it strikes me. The dead were borne in a horse-drawn wagon with a few fellow workers following along, up London Road, up the hill that today peters out into a path. One or more men would have been sent ahead to dig the grave. They would have lowered the pine box—or just a body in a shroud—said a few words, maybe said they'd get word home to Cork. No priests, no last rites, and the shame of burial in unconsecrated ground. The first mass was said in Patrick Burns's shanty south of Keene as the railroad approached, but it was more than a dozen years before the first parish. Someone would have ranged along the stone wall and come back with a stone. And that's it." I wiped my hands and said, "'*Back to work boys. Back to work.*' They hopped on the wagon and rode downhill to continue the workday, blasting and moving granite."

"I wonder if they were laying them to rest knowing or believing they wouldn't be visited, so why take the trouble to memorialize them to posterity," Henry said.

"Or were these stubby stones a promise to return and place a proper headstone?" I asked. "No way of knowing."

"I wonder if there were any way to get word back to their families?" Steve asked.

"Someone might have written home if they were literate, but many weren't," I said. We discussed how a family would have gotten word. Many of the Irish came to America in families: "You'd send word down to where you were hired in Boston or New York. And someone would tell someone, who would tell someone else. Maybe. But it's the signal mark of emigrating that your family falls off the edge of the earth. They disappear."

Steve went over to a stone wall, where he took out his guitar and played quietly, as if tuning. He played a tune, "The Road Home," which he had written in memory of his friend, a fellow musician, David Surette. They'd played together for thirty years.

"Well, that's it. That's what the guys here never got to do, the return they were denied," I said.

I read out the names of the men from Cork who were brought to court: "Murphy, Sullivan, Collins. . . ." Were they here? Did the men—and maybe women buried here—did they know them? Of the hundreds of Irishmen who had labored at the summit, they are the only names that survive.

Then Henry offered to read from a poet he had brought along, Patrick Kavanagh.

"Kavanagh? Where's he from—which county?" I asked.

"Monaghan, I think," Henry said.

We stood for a moment, trying to conjure a map of Ireland, looking forward as if the map hung in front of us. Kavanagh, a great poet, was from the North; he was a Far Downs. The Cork men lying beneath us would have to accept him.

Henry read from "The Great Hunger":

> Clay is the word and clay is the flesh.

An airplane passed overhead. Loud, roaring.

> Christ will meet them at the end of the world,
> the slow and the speedier.
> But the fields say: only Time can bless.

Another plane roared overhead. A crow called. It was unusually noisy.

And the grief and defeat of men like these peasants
Is God's way—maybe—we must not want too much
To see. . . .
O let us kneel where the blind ploughman kneels
And learn to live without despairing.

A sapsucker sang. Henry, an astute birder, didn't miss it.

Patrick Maguire, the old peasant,
can neither be damned nor glorified;
The graveyard in which he will lie will be
just a deep-drilled potato-field
Where the seed gets no chance to come through
To the fun of the sun.
The tongue in his mouth is the root of a yew.
Silence, silence. The story is done.

Steve stepped closer and off the cuff sang out a line of a folk song about building the "railways" in the 1840s. Henry knew "Working on the Railway." "I sang that as a kid," he said and joined in:

In eighteen hundred and forty-six
The gang pelted me with stones and bricks,
I was in a hell of a fix
Working on the railway.

I listened and pointed out that *railway* was the British word. They built railways over there; we built railroads. And when the verse came to "stones and bricks," that was a report, across the years of the Irish riots, with the bricks added for the rhyme. The old "provincial spleen" lived on in a song.

We stood in silence. Steve surprised us by offering a poem he had written for our visit, "American Wake." He asked Henry to read it:

They've been sleeping in the ground
a century and a half,
the woods grown up around

these Irishmen
Calloused hands gone to earth
forgotten bones
and unmarked stones

They were peasants who came from a world contained in the small circumference of maybe a dozen miles—a few families, a few roads and fields, homes and pubs, churches and fairs. They knew it deeply; they knew it to be confining, but mostly it was just what they knew. It was the world.

They came to America—been pushed out—forced to make a long passage, more than a month at sea. They came seeking what everyone wants—a start in life, a fair chance, a little happiness. Their lives came to an end down the hill, working on the railway. And here they were, in what was, in their day, a far corner of town, and is now a retired cemetery at a dead end.

The stones are an invisible monument. We expect stones in a cemetery to speak to us. Just up the hill is an early marble headstone, Dr. Noah Fuller, Sr. "Died Apr. 29, 1809 Æt. 70." We don't know if Noah was a good doctor. We don't know what his practice was like. We don't even know if he was a good person. But we have a name and a date. We may never know more than his name, lifespan, and what a country doctor did in the early republic, but we know a doctor is buried here. For the Irish workers, we have only granite scored by the weather, each stone worn into its own topography, each unyielding. Their stones are as silent as the stone walls they were taken from.

We don't know who among the thirty or more Irish buried here died in an accident, or died fighting his fellow countrymen. There is no way to sift and sort the victimhood: Where are the English landlords whose "rack rents" and evictions led to their leaving? And where are the Americans who denied them any other work? Are any of these dead the Corkonians who rampaged in the shanty village and fired at the militia, or were they killed in a rockslide or an explosion? Here lie hardship and hatred, high hopes and ill fortune.

In the old order, the living and the dead never parted. The living kept the dead near, and the dead watched over the living. They walked with their ancestors. If a peasant was asked who he was, he would name his ancestors. He lived where they had lived; his life continued their lives.

Here the dead are forgotten. They're even shunned by the other dead in this small burial ground. They're adrift from their ancestors and their descendants. Back home in their village, everyone was related; back home, the fields, trees, and rocks had names. There were spirits in the land, fairies, peaceful and malevolent tricksters. Here the stones have no names. These Irish dead have no names. They were nameless beyond the railroad's Irish shanty village, and they were nameless in death. "Name unknown." "A whole herd of Irishmen" is buried here.

The Southwest Burying Yard is a *fóidín mearaí*—Irish for "the stray sod," a place where we go astray, lose the path, fall into a spell, wander lost between what is flesh and what is spirit. For the Irish who advertised, desperate to find their lost children and siblings, America was a *fóidín mearaí*.

Steve took out his fiddle to play a traditional tune, "The Star of the County Down"—a tune from a county further north than Kavanagh's—one of the northernmost counties in Northern Ireland. We'd gone north beyond even the Far Downs.

Henry read again from Kavanagh, a short poem, "Epic." It ends,

Till Homer's ghost came whispering to my mind.
He said: I made the *Iliad* from such
A local row. Gods make their own importance.

A lifetime of striving and strife, an *Iliad* lay beneath our feet.

We had offered our songs and poems. "And that is what a 'ceili' is: the conjunction of proper quiet with proper noise, the exchange of wordless and wordy gifts," says Henry Glassie. "In ceilis, food and stories are given, taken, traded."

We had given our wordless and wordy gifts. We stood a moment in proper silence. We opened the tall cans of Guinness. I offered a toast: "To the Irish, so far from home." The beer was sweet and wet, was life. In a whisper, I said again, "So far, far from home." I took another sip.

PART III

"THERE IS A PRESENCE IN WHAT IS MISSING."

A portrait of Lieutenant Sanderson Sloane presides over weddings at his memorial, the Cathedral of the Pines. PHOTO COLLAGE.

HOMECOMING DENIED

Douglas and Sybil Sloane and their four children were looking for a summer place in 1937, one that wasn't too far from Boston. They'd looked at a lot of houses, some near the New Hampshire state line, but that was already far enough. They didn't want to look at anything in New Hampshire, it was just too far. Their real estate agent managed to drag them across the state line to Rindge. They got out of their car, and before even looking in the house, they walked uphill to an old hayfield, and there was a view that took in the three ponds that almost encircled the Hales' "Interlaken Farm."

They were sold. "There was no dickering over the price, not even a 'walking of the bounds,'" said Douglas. The Sloanes bought the Hale farm, 128 acres with a big farmhouse and the hayfield, the "five-acre piece mowing" that six generations of Hales had tended since 1760. They wanted their four children to join them and let each one pick out a few acres. The oldest, Doug, chose an old cabin by Emerson Pond; the youngest son, Jack, picked out land near that cabin. Daughter Margaret weighed her choices. The second-oldest son, Sanderson (Sandy), chose land up above the farmhouse and the hayfield, a spot where the family would witness sudden, great change. A gap in the stone wall led to a stand of white pine so thick the trees darkened the path.

Walkers could only see a few feet ahead, that is until the hurricane of 1938 blew apart the forest. In an era of limited forecasting, before storms had names, the hurricane arrived unannounced in a New England that believed it was immune to visits from tropical storms. No warning, no preparation. "Thirty-Eight"—that's what they called it for decades after—was devastating, one of the worst disasters in American history, surpassing the San Francisco earthquake in death, injury, and destruction. Thirty-Eight left scars psychological and physical—in the woods, in places, eighty-five years later, you can still see fallen trees. It was a "wind to shake the world," a wind that remade the Hale farm.

The mighty storm revealed an amazing view of Mt. Monadnock, the presiding eminence, the Mountain That Stands Alone, the hub to so many spokes. On Sandy's knoll, he was lifted up as he faced the mountain, as if he were in the palm of a hand, as if he was flying toward and over the mountain. He'd build his home here, he said, and start his life with his wife, Margaret (Pegs), and their son.

Pegs was the girl next door, a close friend of his younger sister. Her family had a summer house on the "next hill over" from the Sloanes. "I must admit that I was smitten" with Sandy, she recalled years later. He was as "handsome as they come!" but she didn't see him much until she was a bridesmaid at Margaret's wedding in 1942. "Then all of a sudden, Sandy, who had by then enlisted in the army, saw me as someone other than the kid next door." They had a "whirlwind romance," were engaged in three weeks, and were married six months later. They were together as Sandy was sent to different bases in the South, training to be a B-17 bomber pilot. Their son was born back home in October. A few weeks later Sandy was sent overseas. He never saw his son.

Sandy was stationed in England, part of the Eighth Air Force's dangerous mission to subdue Nazi Germany. He named his plane *Peg-O-My-Heart*, an old popular song from the Ziegfeld Follies. On his fourteenth mission, February 22, 1944, returning from bombing an aircraft factory, *Peg-O-My-Heart* was hit by anti-aircraft flak over Koblenz, Germany. The plane caught fire, spiraling down to crash in a forest. Sandy and all but one of his crew was killed. His return was thwarted, his homecoming denied. He was twenty-seven years old.

A couple of months earlier, a war correspondent had met a pilot in England who was forced down in bad weather miles from his airfield after a mission to Bremen, Germany. "I came upon him hunched up over a small stove," Arch Whitehouse wrote about Sandy. "He was still encased in his bulky altitude equipment." Most everyone else had already changed into a clean uniform, but Sandy "sat there quiet and unseeing.

. . . Someone had handed him a mug of hot coffee, but it trembled and slopped over as he held it on his knee." Whitehouse had "met hundreds like him. . . . Just another American boy, a long way from home and Christmas Eve only a few hours away." Sandy didn't want to talk; he didn't want to go to the dance just down the hall.

Whitehouse pressed on, asking him about his background. When Sandy mentioned New Hampshire, it was like he'd set off a flare. Whitehouse was from New Hampshire; Sandy was the first American overseas he'd met from his home state. "The change that came over Sandy was startling. . . . He sat up straight and stared at me like a man from another world."

"When you go home," Sandy said,

> *go up and see my knoll. It's right near our house. Remember the hurricane of 1938? Well, it's just as if God had taken a hand in the making of it. Just as though He had finished something that had slipped His mind. My knoll used to be guarded by giant pines, and it was like walking into a great green cave, but the big wind came and blew most of the trees down. For weeks we didn't dare go up and examine the damage. We all felt sick about it. But we had to face it, and one late spring morning, we—Dad and Mom and I—walked up. Instead of the destruction we expected, there stretched before us the most beautiful view God ever put together. No one had ever seen that view before because of those big trees. Only the small ones on the crest were left, and they spread their branches and formed an emerald arch through which we looked down on Bullet Pond and Grassy Pond, Mount Monadnock and the whole Monadnock Divide. Off to one side is Temple Mountain and, past it, the Packs and Crotched and the rolling hills all the way to Mount Kearsarge. And over to the west, through the saddle between Little Monadnock and Gap Mountain, you can see the green hills of Vermont.*

"When you see Dad," Sandy continued, "tell him not to touch my knoll until I get back. One of these days I'm going to build something there. Something worthwhile. Maybe only a cabin, maybe a house. I don't know what, but it will have to be right. Maybe I shouldn't even touch it," he said. "It's just like a cathedral."

Once he got home, Whitehouse visited the Sloanes to bring them news of their boy. Two days later a telegram arrived. Sandy was missing in action.

Time stopped for the Sloanes. Their youngest son, Jack, who had also enlisted and flew many missions as the pilot of a smaller B-26 bomber, completed his tour and came home. On Sandy's "cathedral" knoll, the pines lay where they had been felled by the hurricane. His parents began sawing, cutting, and burning piles of limbs and branches. They began where Sandy was going to build his house, by themselves at first through the winter, left alone to stare into the pyre. In summer their neighbors joined them, and slowly they untangled the fallen trees, clearing a space. On the last Sunday in August 1945, with the war over, at the "most beautiful view God ever put together," the family held a memorial service for Sandy. The town's selectmen pitched in, loaning the benches from the town hall to be trucked to the grove. Three ministers from nearby churches and 127 friends and neighbors came and waited out a downpour before the service.

Later, their neighbors began to call the Sloanes to ask if they could hold a funeral service there for someone in their family. The place spoke to them. The Sloanes had been planning a small memorial. Long before they came to New Hampshire, Douglas had wanted to build an outdoor chapel. They thought about the families who had asked to pray on their hillside. Maybe that's what they were meant to do: open their farm to console others. And there, where Sandy and Pegs never got to build their home, the family began the Cathedral of the Pines. They did their best to restart the clock.

On through the fall and a winter when it hit twenty below zero, the Sloanes had a growing crew of men to finish clearing the knoll. Some stopped by just to see what was going on, and "before they knew it, they, too, were hauling rock." Seth Cleaves and his blind mare "did heroic work." A local mason, "Old" John Crosby, and his two helpers began building a stone altar using rocks from the hayfield, the Hales' harvest of 177 years. Cleaves, his mare, and Crosby paused for photos. They have good, honest faces. The list of workers, paid and volunteer, neighbors and friends, kept growing. They buried wires to bring in electricity and donated hymnals and sheet music. They gathered for "an old-fashioned Bee" to assemble two hundred benches. It was like a barn raising. Building this memorial was one way to leave behind the last fifteen years, to leave behind the hard times of the Great Depression, the punishing winds of Thirty-Eight, and the war years. Easter sunrise services drew as many as 8,000 worshippers, with 175,000 attending through the summer, so many that the state opened a park nearby for picnics.

In addition to the altar, the Sloanes planted two more rocks: One that looks like the gable end of a roof, that sign of shelter that is like interlocking fingers, is on the site of Sandy's house. The other is a stone the family had been carrying around for years. It looks like the open pages of a large bible. That stone tops the lectern. One more stone was brought by a visitor. The lord mayor of Koblenz, Germany (where Sandy's plane had crashed), presented an ancient stone from a city bridge, one that had been destroyed when Koblenz was leveled by Allied bombing. Douglas accepted the gift, with one hand touching the mayor's hands.

I had visited the Cathedral of the Pines not long after we moved to a neighboring town forty years ago. This was in the early days of our arrival, when you stop and look at everything, visit every "attraction" in the tourism bureau brochures. The Cathedral of the Pines seemed like an overreach, a sincere effort that was short of its aspirations. It was more chapel-sized than cathedral. The outdoor church was enclosed by pines that weren't ready for their close-up. They were ordinary. The pines were fifty years old, and most were maybe sixty feet tall. The name promised something grand, like standing amid a grove of California's redwoods. Beyond the Altar of Nations, which was a patchwork of stones from fifty states, there was a view toward Monadnock. It was a good view, one you'd prize if it was on your land, but nothing exceptional. The rows of brown benches looked saggy and awkward, like an earnest Eagle Scout project built for a Boy Scout camp. I felt a little mean-spirited for not liking it. I didn't go back.

At a reading I did for one of my books, the one about my father in World War II, a former trustee for the cathedral, Don Upton, came up to have his book signed and politely insisted that I had to visit. He gave me his card. A few months later, I met him there. Don began by taking me downstairs to a museum, a well-designed space that was about the size of a suburban basement. He stopped before each exhibit, talking about it in detail. He knew the war and the toll it took. The war with its lottery of loss and luck, death and escape, had weight in his telling. He narrated the exhibits for two hours. He was an evangelist for this cathedral of memory.

The story of World War II, as shown in this small museum, is primarily one of a few families and their losses. There are many models of airplanes, uniforms, letters, and official and unofficial tokens of the war.

Sandy's air force footlocker is here, stuffed with the letters that he and Pegs sent back and forth, hundreds of air mail envelopes edged in red, white, and blue, still looking urgent ("*I adore you . . .*"). Above the letters are telegrams. I leaned in close to the glass, just able to make out the faded lines:

> THE SECRETARY OF WAR DESIRES ME TO EXPRESS HIS DEEP REGRET THAT YOUR HUSBAND FIRST LIEUTENTANT SANDERSON SLOANE HAS BEEN REPORTED MISSING IN ACTION SINCE TWENTY TWO FEBRUARY OVER GERMANY PERIOD IF FURTHER DETAILS OR OTHER INFORMATION ARE RECEIVED YOU WILL BE PROMPTLY NOTIFIED PERIOD

How many times did Pegs read that over?

Ten long months later, another telegram:

> REPORT NOW RECEIVED FROM THE GERMAN GOVERNMENT THROUGH THE INTERNATIONAL RED CROSS STATES YOUR HUSBAND SECOND LIEUTENANT SANDERSON SLOANE WHO WAS PREVIOUSLY REPORTED MISSING IN ACTION WAS KILLED IN ACTION TWENTY TWO FEBRUARY NINETEEN

FORTY FOUR OVER GERMANY THE SECRETARY OF WAR EXTENDS HIS DEEP SYMPATHY CONFIRMING LETTER FOLLOWS

That letter is in the glass case, along with a third telegram:

CREMATED REMAINS OF THE LATE 1ST LT SANDERSON SLOANE ACCOMPANIED BY AN ESCORT ARE SCHEDULED TO LEAVE NEW YORK ON TRAIN NUMBER FIFTY NEW HAVEN RAILROAD AT EIGHT FIFTEEN

That last telegram arrived four years after the one confirming that Sandy was killed. It takes a long time for a war to end.

We were downstairs in the museum a long while. I felt the war closing in on me. Of all the millions killed and wounded, of all the battles, goodbyes, farewells, and reunions, this is what remained.

I made this note in my small notebook:

How do we find a place in the landscape for memory?
How do we place memory—create a place holder, a memory holder?

And

Can we create a sacred place?

At last we emerged into the ease of a June day and walked to the outdoor cathedral. It had changed since I was last there. Most of the pines were gone. Another big storm had revealed what Sandy Sloane had first seen. The ice storm in December 2008 had toppled the pines, just as the hurricane of 1938 had. The ice storm was the worst natural disaster in the state's history; more than half of New Hampshire sat in the dark and cold for as long as two weeks. The cathedral lost about two hundred big pines. There were jackstraw piles of ice-coated trees heaped on each other, pulling down wires, barricading roads. They had a massive mess to clean up. But when they were done, and they had landscaped, the cathedral was bigger. It hovers, it seems to me; it levitates toward Monadnock. It's as if you were on an altar before Monadnock. Once again airborne, it is a perfect tribute to a pilot. The ice storm was a restoration, clearing what had become enclosed, bringing us back to the place Sandy loved.

The Cathedral of the Pines is a monument to an absence—to the son who never returned. It's a monument to an ache, to a wound that would never heal. Monuments to absence upset us. They don't offer an ending. There's no escape.

The tendency is to keep adding things to such monuments—statues, flags, words inscribed in stone. At many memorials, they only obscure, but not here. For more than seventy-five years, people have been bringing things to the cathedral. They've sent hundreds of stones from their home place, donated their uniforms and medals. It's like the flowers left at the Cenotaph and the letters and dog tags left at the Vietnam Veterans Memorial.

People show up at times of stress—the day after the attacks on 9/11—and in times of joy, for weddings, graduations, the occasional baptism, and sunrise services on Easter morning. They swarm in on motorcycles for the Blessing of the Bikes. Veterans make pilgrimages to the cathedral. Each vet who visits, in groups or by themselves, brings a memory. It's as if they brought a small stone to leave behind. Everything here—the stones from different states in the altar, the museum displays—is about building a shelter for memory. Bring your grief, your remembered joy, the feeling you can't even describe—the cloud of passing remembrance—bring it here. It takes thousands of acts of dedication to make a place sacred. That, anyway, is my theory while I stand next to Don, looking toward Monadnock.

What had pressed in on me in standing before the museum's exhibits was something like the Doppler effect, the way sound and light is distorted as it races toward us and then away. We hear it any time an ambulance, siren on, speeds past us. The history of World War II is fast receding from us. Of the sixteen million Americans who had served in that war, fewer than fifty thousand remain, just enough to fill a good-sized stadium. Not long from now, there will be only a few hundred living veterans. And the next day we'll be on our own.

Standing before the black-and-white photos and uniforms behind the glass, our hearts still beat. Behind the glass were lives that had taken their last breaths in the 1940s. Life on our side of the glass is insistent. It must go on.

Sandy says goodbye to his pregnant wife. Pegs goes home to live with her parents. Sandy is gone only three months when the telegrams begin arriving: missing in action, killed in action, cremated remains being shipped home. Pegs is a war widow with a baby. Not long after, her father dies. Then her son, only two years and seven months old, dies from pneumonia. Sanderson Sloane Jr. is buried with his father on the Sloanes' farm, the cathedral grounds. Pegs and her mother still come to their summer cottage; she's forever a part of the Sloane family. She picks out the site for the altar and is there to help almost daily. On one visit she meets a volunteer at the cathedral. He had been Sandy's high school classmate; they ran on the track team together. Ten years after Pegs lost Sandy, she marries. She has three more children. The war is over. Life goes on. It has to.

This is what is behind all monuments: Life flows on. Different and ever different waters flow down, as Heraclitus said. Everything is change. Or as poet Robert Hass said, there are no nouns. It's all verbs. It's all about becoming. As Hass said one day teaching a class, "If everything is constantly changing, that means, for example, that *a noun is a lie*. That there's no such thing as a tree as an essential entity. There's a bunch of chemicals out there that are treeing; they're doing the thing. It's an action. Language puts into nouns what is only verbs, because the world is a verb. There is nothing but action, nothing but change."

It's all change. So what are we to do with all these stones of remembrance, our eternal memory holders? At days' end we have great faith that these memorial stones, these nouns, will speak for us. A monument may be a noun; our tribute is the verb. The Cathedral of the Pines—and all memorials—are but a moment, an island in the stream, a rock washed over by all our lives.

In the local paper one week, on the wedding page, I notice a photo of a young couple who have married at the Cathedral of the Pines. They embrace in front of a painting of Lieutenant Sanderson Sloane.

FALLING FROM A FERRIS WHEEL

I.

The summer I turned five years old, a man, his pregnant wife, and their small daughter fell from a Ferris wheel in our town. At the top of the wheel, the door on the gondola, the small car they were riding in, flapped open, the car turned upside down, and they were pitched out. The adults were thrown onto the other gondolas. Their daughter hit the pavement six stories below.

They were taken to the hospital, a small one that three doctors had recently opened just up the hill. The girl died; she was two and a half years old. The couple lived, as did their unborn daughter. They were in the news briefly. There was the shock of the accident, a state inquiry, a grand jury, and then the story disappeared.

The Ferris wheel accident was the end of the small amusement park. Harvey's Fairyland had about five or six rides and a flat-topped shed that sold hamburgers and French fries. It was one of the many small family businesses that rose with the booming new suburbs on Long Island in the decades after World War II. They were homemade roadside attractions, just a notch up from someone's hobby in the basement. Harvey's wasn't much, but for a mom at home with a toddler or two while her husband was at work, it was enough.

Harvey's was shunned after the accident. The Ferris wheel stopped. Everything else for miles around was only one story tall. The Ferris wheel had the horizon to itself; it was a landmark. It sat there for years, unmoving, rusting, the once-festive yellows, blues, and reds fading, chalky, a memorial and a warning to all who remembered what had happened there. It looked like a child's forgotten toy.

That summer, sometime shortly before my fifth birthday, my mother was taken to a hospital for months. We all have our personal, private monuments—places that hold the memories of important moments. Childhood leaves behind a landscape of invisible monuments. The unturning wheel became my monument to that summer. The family's fall from the Ferris wheel and my mother's absence has been banded together in my memory forever, but five-year-olds, it turns out, are not reliable historians.

My mother had been walking in the rain and had gotten very sick, so sick she had to leave for months, my father told his two sons, ages five and ten. She had pneumonia, he said, a big word for a little kid to take in. It did its job; I never doubted. My father would go to the furthest lengths to let children be children. He believed in childhood.

I'm sure that when my friends asked, "Where's your mom?" I said, "She has pneumonia." It wasn't until I was in my late forties that I realized the obvious, and only after my wife told me that's not how you get pneumonia and that's not why she was sent to the hospital. In my defense, I can only say that the youngest child of a family is in a poor position to know what's going on. It's not that I'm an unreliable narrator, but rather an easily deceived narrator, one who will believe a thin lie for thirty-five years.

We visited the hospital a couple of times. I recall waiting outside, but my brother David says that we were allowed to see our mom. The hospital had small white cottages ringing a common park. While my mother was there, she sewed me a stuffed brown dog made of felt and a pajama holder in the shape of a round rabbit and maybe some other things. I kept the brown dog for many years, until its long ears fell off and its felt body was so thin that it fell apart.

A couple of years ago, the name of the hospital came up, and though I hadn't heard it mentioned since I was a boy, I snapped to attention immediately upon the mention of Brunswick Psychiatric Hospital. My brother remembers a Dr. Riley, a psychiatrist, coming to the house at night. Bad times he didn't want to think about, he said. I don't recall Dr. Riley, but again the name is familiar, some kind of memory hiding in the dark.

The summer of my earliest memories is dry and hot. A drought left yellowed and browned lawns that were spiky to walk across in bare feet. Restaurants were forbidden to serve glasses of water unless you asked. We set out sprinklers—the kind that swept back and forth with waving arms of water—and ran through. We ate popsicles and those frozen ices in long plastic sleeves and waited for the ice cream man.

We were left to ourselves outside all day, sometimes drowning in boredom, sometimes riding bikes, sometimes adventuring in the woods and fields or joining up with other kids for games of baseball and kickball. Nothing happened except the increasing hum of the crickets as August came on and the rising of the fireflies at night. We watched cartoons like *Bugs Bunny* on black-and-white TVs and reruns like *I Love Lucy*. Fathers were gone all day at work. Mothers were home, not always visible but usually present. Sometimes you went to the beach, sometimes out to eat, or to the movies with banners advertising "air-conditioned" in ice-covered letters. It was a kid's summer, an eternity, a vast sun-heated plain. The summer the Ferris wheel stopped and my mother went away was one of my happiest, most memorable summers, but that's like recalling a summer day without turning around to see the dark clouds of a thunderstorm coming in.

My Grandma Ida, my father's mother, came out from the city to look after us. She was a short woman (even to a little kid) from the "Old Country," Lithuania, who would break into runs of speaking Yiddish, often with my father so we wouldn't understand. She smoked a lot, moved around the house briskly in a sack-like house dress, and walked to get groceries a half-mile away, pulling a small, upright cart that she must have brought with her from the city. No one else in our neighborhood had a cart like that.

That summer, Chubby Checkers's hit, "The Twist," was still going strong. Grandma Ida loved "The Twist." She returned from one of her shopping trips with a record in a light green sleeve. She played it a lot as she did housework, and the record and the ancient cart, two more invisible monuments, resided in our house until neither of my parents lived there anymore.

Our close neighbors, the Schwartzes and the Davies, loved Ida. They joined her in looking after us. We often ate lunch outside at the picnic table in the Davies' backyard with their boys, dipping peanut butter and jelly sandwiches in chocolate milk and playing with "whistle pops" for dessert, a big lollipop that you could play as you ate it. My memory is that Mrs. Schwartz and Mrs. Davies were in and out of our house many times a day.

For my fifth birthday, Grandma Ida and Aunt Sylvia, my father's older sister, and other relatives rallied around to throw me a big party. Aunt Sylvia had rescued her younger brother another time when Mom was absent, adding my brother, who was still sleeping in a crib, to her Brooklyn apartment with her young daughter and son.

I was saved by my father, my grandma, my aunt, other aunts and uncles, and our neighbors. How do you pay that back, or can you even pay that forward? Something like survivor's guilt is what I feel—I'm in a lifeboat; we're rowing away as the ship sinks. The guilt is all engulfing. I think now, that summer may be the crucible of who I am.

I didn't know what was really wrong with my mother. It was just another mystery that belonged to adults. "Pneumonia" was its own kingdom. No one ever sat us down and said, "You know, your mother has problems." No one ever said, "Your mother is depressed," or any other such words. My father would say, "Your mother is going to be okay." And my mother would ask him, "Am I going to be okay?" Or she'd ask, "I'm okay, right?"

a refrain that increased in her old age. My father carried the weight; he was determined to carry us all.

We were rocked by her long absence, by her sadness. After her return, I started first grade. At recess I stuck close to the teacher on the playground. Standing next to her, I leaned back against a brick wall and rested on my palms. I can still remember the prickly feel of those bricks—they didn't have a smooth face. I did eventually venture out to the big playground.

My brother, starting fourth grade, found excuses to be sent to the school nurse, Mrs. Murphy. He was visiting Mrs. Murphy so much that the school had to call my parents. He was an engaging talker. He knew about baseball, hockey, politics, some Motown hits, and weather forecasting. He could hold an adult's attention.

For all the care that everyone took with us, we were, in our childhood ways, trying to fill in what was missing. No one explained depression to children or teens then, and it's a word that we never used in our house. That subject was like Hawaii. For 250 years European explorers had sailed past it, many miles away, before they found it, or so I've read. The same is true for Mom's troubles. We sailed around it, but we never landed.

I have long thought that I have an especially acute memory of that summer, that I was an eagle-eyed five-year-old, a scribe in training, but it turns out that we did the same few things over and over. I have a witness. In my late twenties, I was home for a visit; I had moved out years earlier. Somehow, I had been roped into cleaning up the basement. In a shoebox of plumbing parts—copper fittings and other bits—I found a short stack of letters that Dad had written to Mom when she was in the hospital. There are seventeen letters, most delivered by hand, usually with a box of cookies from her favorite Italian bakery, Collette's. He traveled a triangular route that summer from home to work, a half-hour; from work to the hospital and then home, an hour. He wrote her almost daily, sometimes twice a day. I don't have all the letters; these seventeen are the survivors. The earliest is from May 11, about a month before my birthday, and the last is from the "dog days of August." These letters are alive for me; they have heat. They're a net thrown into the ocean, a catch of days that would have disappeared as they were lived. I never casually pick them up, and if our house were to burn, I'd grab them first.

In the letters, Dad with his "Ma" is taking us to small amusement parks many times. Dad and David play miniature golf while I'm on the rides with Grandma Ida. Another night she takes me roller skating when David has a baseball game. We all go for "malted milk shakes." We swim at the beach. We watch the airplanes at Zahn's, a small, grass-strip landing field that Dad liked. (Grandma says the planes are too small; she'd never get in anything with only one motor.) We go shopping for pants, sneakers, and shirts at Korvette's, a department store, over and over. Korvette's was like our second home. I think Dad found its ordered aisles of budget-priced plenty reassuring. He buys my brother a new baseball mitt for his Little League games and a long-promised bicycle. Grandma buys me a puppet (perhaps the tiger puppet I kept always). No wonder I remember this as a good summer.

He keeps Mom apprised of the goings-on at home, the tomatoes we planted, the outdoor faucet he's putting in, my brother and his friend mowing the backyard to earn fifty cents, the "women in the neighborhood . . . bellowing for their children to come in for supper." The lilacs are blooming, and "of course, the pride of the block, our flowering crab, is just a myriad of blossoms." In the evening, Mr. Davies and Mr. Schwartz just happen to stop by, and they "shoot the breeze" over a beer. Mrs. Schwartz takes Ida out shopping so she can have a night off. She and her husband come over to keep Ida company during a loud thunderstorm. (They share a "fear of thunder and lightning.") Mrs. Davies takes her brood and my brother to Jones Beach, while Ida watches the Davies' youngest son and me. She packs the older boys off to the movies so they can cool off (a double feature: *Frances the Talking Mule* and *Abbott and Costello Meet Dr. Jekyll and Mr. Hyde*). Grandpa Elai comes out for a few days so Ida can return to the Bronx. Aunt Sylvia and Uncle Irving frequently stop by, or have us spend Memorial Day with them in Brooklyn, or take me and my brother to the zoo.

The adults here are heroic. They are building an ark for two boys and their father. They show up again and again. They shepherd us in this rough crossing.

My brother and I are deep in summer's freedom. The letters report our childhood chatter: my brother going into lavish detail about a forecast thunderstorm, drawing such a dire picture—hail and tornadoes—"that if it all happened as forecast then we had better start building an ark." And I'm apparently a "yakker." "From the time he awakes till bedtime its yak, yak, yak. Sometimes he talks in his sleep too!! But he's a gem, and, of course, so is David."

He loves all that, but he misses her, dropping off letters daily, visiting when he's allowed on the weekends, usually both days. Sometimes Dr. Riley and another doctor won't let him visit. Otherwise, the letters have no medical details.

He encourages her, telling her the great things they'll do when she returns. They'll take some trips, refurnish the house, go to the parks, beaches, and restaurants they both love. "Plans for all of us include the good times we have every summer." He mentions cookouts at Crab Meadow Beach, Fire Island, and Jones Beach. They'll visit a big garden in Tuxedo, New York, that he read about in a brochure. "We are hoping you will get well soon and come home to us so we can do all those things together." Life will resume when she's better. He has "arranged to postpone" his "vacation indefinitely." Instead, he'll work overtime. "That'll be our vacation money." In the meantime, don't worry about him. "Forget it. I'm concerned, not worried," he says, drawing a fine distinction.

In the first letter I have from May 11, he sounds like he's still in shock:

> *The boys and I miss you terribly. However we are slowly making adjustments.*
>
> *I am certain the people in this hospital can and will help you to a speedy recovery. Just give them time, patience and cooperation. . . . I miss you very much. It just isn't the same. I keep myself busy both at work and at home. When you come home we'll have to go out to dinner like we always do. I miss that.*

He signs it with his nickname: "Love, Pinky." (His first name was Pincus.)
David writes to her in wobbly script,

> *Dear Mom,*
> *I hope you will be home soon.*

He then tells her about his new bicycle, which is black and white with whitewall tires and "carrier clamps for the paper. . . . Love, David."

And I have made her a present: "Howard wants me to let you know that he found the clay man he made you and has it in safekeeping for you."

She wrote back but only a couple of times from what I can tell, once not long after she was there. Dad treasured her letter. He replied, "I've read it several times. It is the most beautiful letter I ever received. It is special to me." I don't have that letter. He continues,

> *Our visit last weekend was the greatest! You looked well and beautiful. No doubt about it, you are well on the road to recovery.*
> *There is nothing I can add that I haven't said already about how important you are to me and what a void there is with you gone. The thought that I'll see you Saturday and Sunday and that you'll be home soon, makes it almost bearable. Bernice, there is nothing but happiness for us! Believe me!*

Toward the end of her stay, the doctors let her come home for weekend visits. "I spoke with Dr. Riley. . . . Things are looking good." He tells her to ask for a "weekend pass," and he will, too.

Listen to the doctors; you'll get better, he says. I love you; you'll get better. If love could cure mental illness, she would have walked free.

II.

They met right after the war. Dad was home from the army air forces. He'd flown nineteen missions as a gunner in a bomber over Germany and France, before he was seriously wounded. He was carried off the plane in a stretcher and spent the next five and a half months in hospitals in

England and the States. But now the war was over. It was peacetime, 1946, and like millions of others, he had to find a job. He was back in his old neighborhood in the Bronx by Claremont Park. She lived with her mother in the same neighborhood and worked as a legal secretary, making a good living.

I don't know how they met, but I have a document of their happiness. When we were cleaning up the house after they died, we came across a photo album we had never seen. The album was from 1946, their first year together. My mom is radiant, movie-star glamorous, a real beauty, a woman who would catch your eye across a crowded room.

The black-and-white photos are tipped into the pages with photo corners. In her perfect schoolgirl script she has written captions in white ink on the black album paper and titled the album, "The Ever-Lovin' Mansfields." Each weekend was an adventure, each had its own title: "Spring Valley Odyssey," "Honeymoon in June," "Darling, You & I, Summer 1946." They took a boat ride with their friends up the Hudson to Bear Mountain ("The Gang's All Here"). They visited Lake Champlain, Fort Ticonderoga, and friends in Rockaway. The men are sharp in pinstriped suits with wide lapels, wide ties, and rakish Fedoras. The women, in long skirts and soaring hats, are regal in a way I've only seen in old movies ("My Man, Myself and New Coat"). Mostly, Mom and Dad pose for the camera: "The Ever Photographin' and Photographed Mansfields." Of course, they weren't yet my parents; they were twenty-one and twenty-two years old in a new world of no hard times and no war. This is what peace looks like.

They were in love; she was delivered from the sour rooms of her childhood. It's a happy story. My father is dashing. He'd been wounded in the war, seen horrible things about which he'd never speak, and now he was alive and in love with a real beauty. And here were all of their friends, his childhood friends who had also come through the war alive, and my mother's friends. It was all good.

One photo from 1946 stood out in my father's memory. He told me about it in his last years. He remembered a spring day when my mother was walking down Nelson Avenue, where they had their first apartment near Yankee Stadium. He was waiting for her. She had on a white dress, white gloves, and a "picture hat"—this, he told me, was a hat that sits like a dish behind the head "like a halo." His father used to make those hats. "She looked elegant."

Standing up on the front steps, he took a picture of her on the sidewalk. He couldn't find it, but he didn't need to. This was how he saw her even into their nineties, when Mom was living apart from him in a nursing home. On one visit, he asked her if she remembered that hat and that day. She couldn't hear him by then; she was deaf.

When he told me about that photo, he said, "She had me from the first."

My mother's life really began when she met my father. She did what she could to leave behind her lonely years, first by changing her name. She was born Esther Feldstein, but by high school, she had chosen Bernice as her first name, and would spend most of her life signing checks as Bernice Mansfield. She had one of the saddest childhoods I've ever encountered. I didn't know this until after she died, and I still don't know that much.

Her father, out of work, destitute in the Great Depression, died while shoveling snow on a make-work project. He was on the dole, put to work by the WPA. As a child, I was told this and only this about my missing grandfather.

It is not true.

Her father is a mystery. I only learned his name when I turned up a passport application and two photos. In one, taken near the end of his life, he looks shifty, the kind of small-time gangster that other gangsters wouldn't trust.

David Feldstein was born in Iasi, Romania, in the Jewish ghetto called the Red Bricks. He had a younger sister who also came to America. His immigration is unusual. He first came to the West Coast. He appears in the 1910 census, living alone as a house painter. He marries and divorces. He shows up next in Seattle, applying for citizenship, declaring his intention to be naturalized. After that I can find no trace of him until he applies for a passport in 1921. When he first came to the country, he didn't need a passport. "The huddled masses" just showed up, usually at Ellis Island, were checked for diseases, and were waved through.

He says that he's a waiter and that he's been living on the Lower East Side since 1914. As his witness, he brings along his friend who is a street sweeper. There's a photo of him looking square into the camera in a rumpled suit that he may have borrowed. One of his sisters had written, pleading with him to come home immediately. He gave the letter, written in Romanian, to the passport official, who made a quick note on his application: "Kindly come and see your Dear mother at least for one more time, etc." The official kept his letter.

Back home in the Iasi ghetto, he met Julius Lazarowitz, a shoemaker with thirteen children. He wanted to marry off his oldest daughter. Julius seemed to think that this waiter from the Lower East Side was rich, and maybe he was when compared with the poverty of the Jews hemmed into the Red Bricks. What little they had was thought by the authorities to be too much.

Julius forced his daughter Sylvia to marry David. He gave her away. Sylvia cried all the way to America, she said. She was forced to leave her "sweetheart." It was a bad match; he was nineteen years older than her. They ended up living with his sister. Sylvia was miserable.

"I would have had a better house in the Old Country," she told my mother.

"What about seeing the Statue of Liberty? Wasn't that exciting?" Mom asked her.

"What statue? I was crying."

Their firstborn daughter, Goldie, died from a burst appendix at two years and eight months. My mother was born the next year, and her brother Gilbert, two years after. Goldie never left the family. They often went to Mt. Judah Cemetery to stand before her gravestone, a black granite pylon topped by a carved lily against a tree stump ("Dear Daughter . . . At Rest"). A big portrait of Goldie sitting on Sylvia's lap was probably the largest photo or art of any kind in their apartment. It's a sweet photo, not a stiff portrait. Mother and child are happy.

"Did your mother talk about that?" I asked Gilbert at a family gathering. He was a reclusive bachelor. I only saw him three times.

"That's *all* she talked about," he said. This lost child cast a spell.

In the late 1920s, as New York City was booming, their fortunes changed. They rose in the world. Her father opened some sort of restaurant. Maybe it was a speakeasy; maybe it was a bar and grill on Fourteenth Street or a Romanian restaurant, which were popular. Famous people went there, I've been told. He played the role of an exotic gypsy, sitting in a grand robe, telling fortunes. His sister was sought out for her fortune telling. She was supposedly very accurate and could foretell events. They were raided by the police for fortune telling—they could be fined or jailed for fraudulent clairvoyance.

They moved out of the Lower East Side to the Bronx, land of the middle class. They had a maid. He drove a Pierce Arrow. He may have been living over his head. He was likely one of those businessmen who would expand on a hunch and risk it all. But at last, he was a success in America. He was, of course, not prepared for what happened next—the Great Depression. He missed it even though he was a fortune teller.

His speakeasy/bar and grill/restaurant closed. He came home that day with a big salami. "This is all that's left," he said. They lost their maid and the fancy car. They moved frequently because they couldn't pay the rent; they were on Home Relief. Sylvia took the kids and left him. My mother was in high school. She was depressed, although I'm sure no one recognized that. The school, seeing how sad she was, wanted to call home to have them come for her. "No," my mother said. "Call my Tanta Becky."

Her aunt was busy raising four boys and one girl, but she managed to look out for my mother. Whatever refuge she found, it was with Tanta Becky. One summer during her high school years, she went to bed for a long time, maybe most of the summer, a hallmark of depression. She only told me this in her last years. Before that, I had no idea of how all alone she had been, with a bitter mother and an absent father.

Her father was still knocking around the neighborhood, a shabby figure who lived in a spare room at the temple and showered at a niece's house. He said he was an "antiques dealer." One winter morning, he had a heart attack and dropped dead in the street. He was sixty-two. He was headed over to his niece's to take a shower. His death certificate listed his "profession" as "junk dealer." David Feldstein didn't have much to show for thirty-six years in America.

He is never spoken of again. He disappears beneath the waves. At all our family gatherings, I don't recall meeting one Feldstein or Feldstein relative. We rarely saw her mother and brother. Her father died on January 6, 1946—not while shoveling snow in the Great Depression. (But he was dead to the family long before he was dead in the street.) The next month, my mother, still dressed for mourning met the man she would marry. Years later she wrote, "Deep down I was relieved that my father was gone. I didn't have to pretend that I had a father anymore."

My mother's favorite book in high school, or so she said in her autograph book, was *The Berry Patch* by Josephine Lawrence. I read one of its many editions.

Four cousins from the city are put on a train to go live with an uncle and an aunt in the country. There are two boys and two girls: One boy is bookish, and one is a prankster who was thrown out of school for some unspecified prank. One girl is very opinionated and loves clothes—she's wearing "dainty white silk gloves" on the train—and the other girl is a slob and a bit of a shambles. The two girls' mothers are in England for the year. They are not happy about being pulled out of their city schools—Miss Saunders School for Girls for the one in white gloves—to go to a "dinky high school." But we know from the first scene that they'll find happiness in the country.

Their uncle is Judge Berry, and his home—"The Berry Patch"—

> *was the best type of Colonial architecture, spacious and dignified, breathing the traditions of courtesy and hospitality from the shining knocker on the white front door to . . . the floors dark with age, the priceless claw-footed mahogany furniture, each piece an heirloom, the ivory finish of the woodwork and window sills and deep fireplaces. . . . No amount of money could hope to purchase the abiding charm of such a house—an American home for generations.*

The home is surrounded by old oaks, elms, and willows, all tended by a loyal handyman.

The Berry Patch must have seemed like Oz to a Bronx girl whose family was on Home Relief. Judge Berry was not a junk dealer. The judge was kind; he takes anyone's case, even if they can't pay. "His name had been a household word for culture and breeding, his position and attainments a matter of affectionate pride." I think my mother longed for someone like the judge. She had a distant relative, an in-law, who became a respected lawyer and judge. Everyone admired Judge Berry, and everyone admired her relative. In her autograph book, she says that her relative is her hero. But above all, the judge, his sister, the help in the house, and a teacher who's also boarding with them pay close attention to the children. Even though the judge goes off to his study and his sister is busy in the kitchen, they are alert to every twitch and concern of the cousins. Attention is love; the cousins are in a safe world.

On one of my visits home, we were driving past Nate Codman's house. He was a crazy kid that I had known a little. He was often in big trouble. One time he spray-painted the junior high school with big letters rendering his verdict on the school principal (he "sucks"). The school was pristine. There was no graffiti anywhere. No one "tagged" street signs, mailboxes, blank walls, or big rocks. Nate got caught. He was in trouble other times, too. He was unstable. Today they'd probably rein him in with drugs.

As we drove past, I asked idly, "Whatever happened to Nate?"

"He got married," my mother said. That's it. Happy ending.

"Why do you think that explains anything?" I asked. "Why do you think getting married means he lived happily ever after?"

I regret saying that. If I were to stand in public, say on the town's common and declare my regrets over all the things I never should have said, I'd be there from sun up to dark, and probably for the next several days, too.

My mother had spoken the truth: Getting married meant living happily ever after. When she met Dad, she was soaringly happy. It was true until it wasn't. I don't know when the fairy tale ended for her, but I know that my mother's demons caught up with her in the summer of 1962.

III.

One night I was shaken out of my sleep by my mother crying. I heard my father, his voice rising, "Bernice, take your pills!" He was pleading with her. "Take your pills!" He was desperate.

"No! No! No!" she said. Her voice was shaky. She was desperate; she was crying. I could hear them moving around the house. Was he chasing her? Maybe. Take your pills. We had a lot of pills in our medicine cabinet. The doctors were throwing darts at a target they struggled to define.

The sadness of that scene hits me full force. My father believing; my mother drowning. My mother crying in the night; my mother in bed all day, many days. All of us acting as if this were normal.

This all came back to me, when in their eighties, he could no longer look after her by himself. He sent her to live in a nursing home. She didn't want to go. (No one wants to leave their home. Most everyone in nursing "homes" is waiting to go home. The next visitor may tell them that their exile has been repealed; their health has been restored, and death shown the door.)

We visited shortly after she had been assigned to the Sea Breeze building. (No sea, no breeze, of course.) She was agitated. Dad took her to talk in an empty room. She lay down in the dark room, facing the wall. He sent me off to wait next door, to wait in another dark, empty room. I could hear him telling her that she was going to be okay. She *had* to do this. "I want to go home," she said. "Why can't I go home?" Dad repeated his reassurances, and she repeated her pleading. Next door in the empty room, I looked out on a worn courtyard, and I was thrown back into my past. I was in my fifties. What does that song say? *You've gone a million miles, but how far did you get?*

My father always thought she'd get better. After a visit to the nursing home, he'd say, "She's doing well, *kinahora*" (invoking the Yiddish phrase to ward off the "evil eye" and protect good fortune). Another time he'd say, "She still has all her marbles." I think that, at times, he mistook a bipolar high, a chattering run, for good health. One Sunday morning when I was home, we went to the bagel bakery for breakfast. That morning, she was focused. We talked with ease. Dad was pleased. "See," he said to me later, "give her a half-hour, and the pill takes effect—your mother's fine." Well, she's not fine, but who has the heart to say that? And it was implied that we were to never come to that conclusion.

We proceeded as if she was okay and also as if she weren't. We received contradictory lectures. We were to treat her normally; we were to treat her with special care. He never said this directly. Nothing direct was said. She's alright; she's not alright. We were caught in a bind. This contradiction tripped us up.

His dedication to her could blind him to everything else. At the nursing home, if he thought she was not being looked after properly or was slighted in any way, he was quick to anger. If I was with him, he demanded that I jump in and pick up the fight. But about what? I had no facts, and this is not the way I talked to people. None of that mattered. I was supposed to march upstairs to the nurses and assume the battle in his angry tone without question.

On her good days, before she was in the nursing home, they lived as if they were still dating. They were still "The Ever-Lovin' Mansfields," vintage 1946. One time I called him on Father's Day and found him in a good mood. They had gone to the marina at Jones Beach for a walk, then to a diner nearby, and on the way home stopped for frozen yogurt.

"That sounds rough," I joked.

"What's that the French say?" he replied. "*Sans souci*," carefree, without worries.

The second year they were married, he made her a birthday card. At his drafting table at work, he sketched her a perfect technical engineering drawing of a toggle switch. Under the switch, in neat letters, "SWITCH TO A HAPPY BIRTHDAY." Was she depressed?

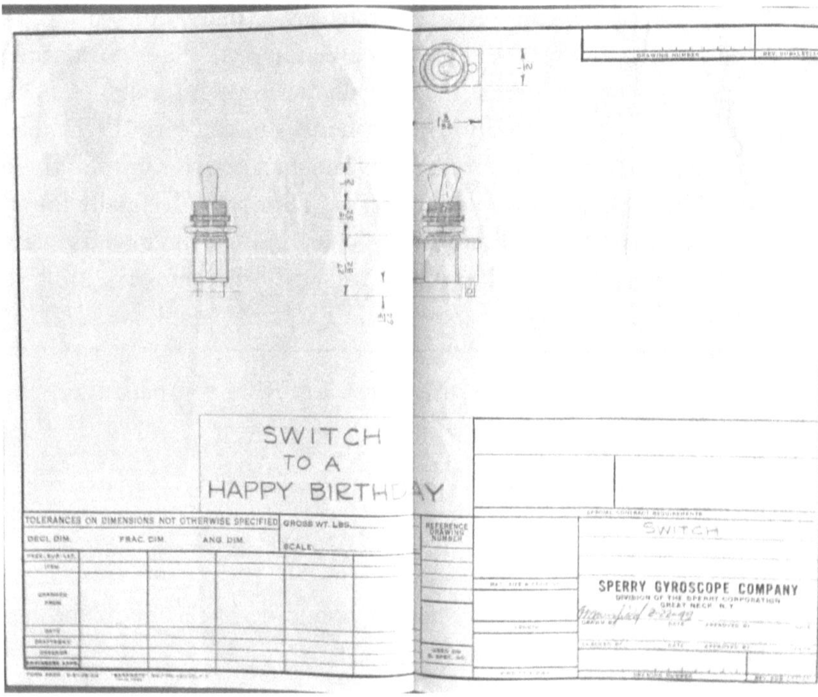

Birthday greeting, February 22, 1949. DRAWING BY PINCUS MANSFIELD.

At his funeral, our rabbi surprised me by asking me to say a few words by the open grave. I'd never been to a Jewish funeral where this was done. Only the Mourner's Kaddish in its haunting, ancient Aramaic is said, and then the mourners come forward to toss a handful of dirt onto the coffin. For those few moments, you are carried along on a river thousands of years old.

I stepped forward, talked briefly about his growing up as a happy city kid, his wartime service when he was nineteen years old, flying in a bomber into harrowing battles, and then meeting Mom. His love never wavered; he always thought she'd get better. I said no more.

Time stopped in my family that summer of 1962. Or maybe time stopped the day my parents met. Maybe it stopped with the idea that my father had to take care of someone. Routine, they say, is one of the core rules for raising children, so maybe there was a benefit. We clung to routine; stasis was my father's achievement, especially when we hit rough patches, like when he was unemployed for many months in the early 1970s. His company, where he'd worked for twenty years, had massive layoffs. There were thousands of engineers looking for the same job. He finally found work—in Connecticut. We didn't move; he commuted three hours every day total, heading through the city and crossing a bridge to arrive on the other side of the Long Island Sound, and then home again. He wouldn't upset my mother.

On another visit home, we drove past a moving van parked on our street.

"Who's moving?" Mom asked.

"I don't know," Dad answered.

"What?"

"*I don't know.*"

"I'm glad we're not moving," she said, sounding like a child. Nothing could change.

Things did go forward—we took family vacations; Dad got his private pilot's license—but this all happened around her depression. I think that he had to check in with her doctors to get the green light to take her away from home.

The summer of 1962 is the fault line. Before and after. I can see it in the old family photo albums. She puts on weight; she looks blank at times. Whatever Dr. Riley prescribed, it didn't work. After that summer, she was still pursued by depression.

IV.

My mom liked to go to the Elwood Diner, which was across the road from the Ferris wheel. I never liked the place. We'd be alone in the diner. I don't think that it was anyone's favorite. We'd walk there. Maybe we'd stop first to get groceries at the Acme, but most likely we'd just "gone out." "Going out" was very important to my mother. She gathered herself to go out, got dressed to look pretty, put on makeup, and then we'd walk the half-mile to the diner, but it felt much longer. This was isolating in itself. No one but kids walked, and even then they were usually on their bikes, but my mother didn't have a driver's license. The whole thing comes back to me as a well of loneliness, walking with my mother as the cars scorched by on Elwood Road. Other times we walked a long way to the doctor or to the temple down a road that had no sidewalks. It felt like we'd fallen out of the world.

Sitting in the diner, I was aware that she was really by herself. She wasn't talking to me, or showing me anything. I was just along. I didn't have words for it then, but she was off by herself much in the way many years later, when she sat by herself in the nursing home, oblivious to all that tumult around her. She'd have coffee—*kawfee*—and an English muffin or a tuna sandwich and check her lipstick by looking into her compact mirror. She was unreachable. She was pleasant enough, but I remember feeling alone at those times. Maybe it's where I began my reporting career—sitting there watching her.

Her depression took her away from us. She loved us; she was never mean. She was proud of us, but through it all, she was lost many days, and some years more than others. She was in her own struggle. If you should only write about what you know, then I should disqualify myself. My mother is someone I know little about, and in her last years, she retreated deeper in a dark woods. She was on a journey away from us, or she was circling, looking for herself, saying often, "I'm going to be alright? Aren't I? Am I going to be alright?"

As Henry James wrote, "There is a presence in what is missing."

Depression is a heavy bondage. It's like living in a dense atmosphere in which one can't move. We love stories; we love riding the "arc" of a narrative. We are forever gathered by the fire, listening to the storyteller's tale that holds back the night and puts the universe in order. Depression defeats narrative. Nothing advances, day after dark day. Alcoholism ruled other families as depression ruled ours.

During one stretch of time in junior high school, when I came home, my mother would send me out to buy bread. I'd walk to the store or ride my bike, and that would take the last little bit of daylight. I don't know how many times I ran this errand. It didn't occur to me until years later, another lifetime it seems, that my mother was supposed to go get that bread. Dad had probably been told by a doctor that she needed a task, an errand, something to get her out of bed, but she didn't. I'd come home, and she was in bed or just up in a nightgown, reading a novel at the kitchen table, and she'd say, "Your father wants you to go get bread."

So that didn't work. No one ever explained this little family play. She did have good days. I remember coming home in the second and third grades, and she was ironing as she watched *The Match Game* on TV. She loved TV, the movies, and novels.

Dad and the doctors tried other tricks. Once a week, she'd take a special bus to go to the "village," which was Huntington. This was a school bus that was routed to stop at the houses of the regulars. She'd buy me clothes. One time it was a shirt. She showed me the shirt. I hated it, and as a junior high school kid would, I told her. She broke down crying and went to her bedroom. I had no idea why.

This was about so much more than a shirt. This was another prescription to give her day meaning, to give it form, a task that would be her North Star. I was in junior high school, how could I know? Yet another regret.

It's the absences that I now total. Looking back, only now do I realize how much I time I spent alone. I was building models in the basement—model cars, trains, rockets, so many models. I was bicycling hundreds of miles in the summer weeks. Only now do I ask myself: Where was my mother?

One morning in elementary school, I was so caught up watching cartoons that I forgot about school, and the bus roared right past our house. We didn't watch TV in the morning in our house. Where was she? She had gone back to bed. She called a neighbor to take me to school.

Left to myself, I was a busy kid; I had many projects. One summer, around the third or fourth grade, I built a weather station like the one pictured in *The World Book Encyclopedia*, a little house with louvered sides, but I only had plywood scraps. Every day, with a clipboard in hand, I'd visit it to record whatever instruments I had set up. I was quite the junior scientist. I was also busy watering the short stalk of a maple tree that I'd rescued from growing by the chimney and replanted. For years it was only a stick. In high school, I stayed after for almost every extracurricular activity there was.

Separation may have been my earliest project—I had to create some distance from her to survive. And her central absence is why, at times, I can intuit the sorrow of others, and why I can also be detached and sarcastic. Sarcasm creates space. It's why as a boy I could see Mr. Scarlatti outside his house, raking his leaves alone, not long after his wife had died, and know that he was lonely. I asked Dad if I should go over and help him. And it's why I never forgot that family falling from the Ferris wheel.

V.

The news reports of the Ferris wheel accident are sparse. There are only four short stories in the local weekly and a news brief in *The New York Times*. When Robert and Joan Shaw and their daughter Deborah got on the Ferris wheel that June day, the wheel's operator, a boy of fifteen, failed to lock the door. On the second rotation, at the top, the door on gondola car 7 opened, catching a bolt on the structure of the wheel. The car flipped upside down, and the family fell through the car's canvas roof. The adults hit the gondolas below. Their daughter fell six stories to the ground. She died of brain injuries. Her parents were hospitalized for "undisclosed internal injuries."

There was an immediate investigation by the Industrial Safety Division of the New York Department of Labor. Two months earlier, in April, there had been another accident when the door of a gondola fell off, bouncing off the ground before hitting an adult on another ride. He was not "seriously injured." The state investigated and said the ride was safe. In May, a month before the Shaws were thrown from the wheel, the ride had passed a state inspection.

The Department of Labor said that the owner of Harvey's Fairyland had broken the law, Industrial Code Part 45, when he allowed a fifteen-year-old to run the Ferris wheel. Operators of amusement rides like that had to be at least eighteen. The Suffolk County DA convened a grand jury, seeking to charge the park's owner with second-degree manslaughter. The grand jury declined to indict him, but said he should be charged for employing a minor to operate the ride.

The Shaws sued the Fairyland at Harvey's—its legal name—for $2 million. Harvey's lawyers fought back, trying to get the suit dismissed for a series of technicalities, most of which were dismissed in the Appellate Division of the state supreme court. And then—nothing, no more news stories. A retired judge I know told me that the family and the insurance company for Harvey's probably settled out of court, leaving no public record. I could find nothing when I filed several requests and appeals under New York's Freedom of Information Law.

Harvey's owner was "heartbroken," his son-in-law told a reporter many years later. Harvey's Fairyland closed not long after, leaving the Ferris wheel as a memorial to the death of a little girl. (The park's miniature golf course persisted, being excused for some reason from the public's boycott.)

Reviewing the record, one fact jumped out at me: The accident happened in 1964, not 1962, the summer my mother went away. I had conflated the two—the lost child, my mother's absence, and my grandmother's arrival. It didn't all happen in the same drought-ridden summer of yellowing lawns, but my memory had sewn the pieces together, making it one story. The chronology is wrong; the memory is compressed, but for me as I grew up, the unturning wheel became the monument to our family, which was stuck in time.

In the end, Pincus Mansfield could not save Bernice Esther Feldstein Mansfield. She went back to a psychiatric hospital for a stay and returned home. Dad told his two middle-aged sons that she had pneumonia. Trying to lift her from her depression was finally too much. He found her a nearby nursing home and visited once or twice a week. "The Ever-Lovin' Mansfields" were sent back to the summer of 1962. She had rough times there, and times when she seemed better.

In her final years, she was on the third floor, which we called the dementia ward. It was hard to visit. Sometimes a patient was crying out in confusion, moaning with crazy complaints, reliving some private drama. It was like hearing only one side of someone shouting into a cell phone. But mostly it was quiet, with some patients watching a blurry old movie on a video screen and others, parked here and there, slumped into their wheelchairs looking like deflating balloons.

We'd find Mom in the big "day room," sitting alone in her wheelchair, pulled up to a table with her book and (empty) pocketbook in front of her. She wasn't reading; she was just sitting there. She lights up when we come in. She is astonished and happy, but distant. She smiles and says, "Howard! I'm so glad." She is the same. Her mind circles, in a loop with one or two worries she can't set aside, but then she breaks the pattern, and she's surprisingly thoughtful, remembering old friends of ours and things we had said on other visits. Those moments of contact, and her happiness when arrive, are the visit.

We usually play many hands of gin rummy, a card game I remember from growing up. Mom is a card cheat; she takes extra turns, and we let her. But some days she lacks enough focus to play cards; she can't follow what's going on, and she wants to be wheeled back to sit by her book and pocketbook to wait for dinner. Some days she's content with our visit, and some days she looks sad and abandoned when we leave.

Occasionally, she has a journal with her where she's trying to write a story she's titled "A Bronx Girlhood." Her once-perfect penmanship has decayed to a line skirting and losing its way across the blank pages, sentences stopping, the same few lines repeating. She wrote,

> *July 21st, 2012: My name is Bernice Mansfield. I remember the Bronx very well. First and foremost, I remember my Tanta Becky.*

This recollection trailed off and would be refrained on other days:

> *This is the story of my Great-Aunt Rebecca. She made my childhood brighter. She was the unsung heroine of my sad childhood. On February 23rd, Washington's Birthday and my birthday, she would stop by the apartment for it. She had my presents all wrapped up.*

And again:

> *For years, on my birthday, she came to wherever I happened to be.*
>
> *Thinking back through the years, I really don't know what I would have done without my Tanta Becky.*

Most of the pages, in journal after journal, are blank. They strike at a writer's heart. It's too accurate of a mind-report. It's too close to what I'm doing now, filling pages with what? I'm running in my maze, and she ran in her maze. Writers' journals are littered with fragments of memory, reprised repeatedly. It's hard to write about herself, she tells me, "it's too revealing."

The absolute worst visit in years of visits was when a nurse gave her a big pink pill she didn't want. She asked that it be cut in half. The ever-patient nurse split the pill. She still refused. "I don't want this," she said, making a sour face. So the nurse mashed it up in pudding. She still didn't want it. The nurse spooned in half of it. My mother was done, she didn't want the rest, but the nurse spooned in the second scoop. As I sat there, I was brought back to that night she was crying when she wouldn't take her pill.

And then we could visit no more. COVID set in; the nursing home was locked down. Every day at 12:30, we received a recorded phone call: "The facility would like to update you about activities in the facility." "With great sadness the facility has experienced a death from COVID-19 today." "The facility continues to take all precautions." These calls were the strangest part of a very strange time. My mom was ninety-four, cut off from all visitors. Dad had died nine months earlier. She was left to herself.

One day it wasn't a recorded call. A nurse was calling. Mom was "declining," she said. Her "dementia had taken over," and she had lost twenty-five pounds. They were trying to get her to eat, but she wasn't interested. "She's not wanting to eat much," she said. This was a sad call, a missed farewell, like arriving at the dock to find that the ship was already out in the harbor, underway.

The next call was the last. My mother had died in the night. The nurse found her in her room at 7:00 a.m. The woman on the phone did say that Mom had spoken of us recently. We had called on Mother's Day, but because of the lockdown, she couldn't come to the phone. They said that they'd relay the message. I think of a nurse's aide poking her head in the door of her room and my mother looking up with that distant look, but taking it in somehow with a bewildered smile. Maybe she was far off and maybe by then, traveling further.

She passed the last two and a half months of her life alone in her room. No one should die like this. I think she was sent back, relentlessly, to the sad rooms of her childhood, to lying alone by herself that summer in high school, but I don't know. Did she despair? Or was it all just the same as sitting alone at the table in the day room? Was she thinking, over and over, "I'm going to be alright. Am I going to be alright?"

Sometime during all those years of visiting my aging parents, the Ferris wheel, landmark of my childhood, vanished. Gone, along with the young suburbs that were awkward in their newness, teeming with baby boom kids and their parents who were freed from the Great Depression and the world war.

For a long time, people remembered the accident: "That's where the baby fell to her death"—for that is how they remembered the little girl. And then even as the steel wheel stood rusting, people forgot. The press of new events and new houses being built and new families moving in washed away the memory. A Fairyland sign stood in tall weeds for decades. Each letter of Harvey's Fairyland was a different color on a white background. The white paint blistered, and the letters faded away, except for the letters in stubborn black paint. Thirty years on, the sign fell over.

Harvey's was torn down, leaving a small, weedy lot. I'd stare at the vacancy—as if it would speak if I stared at it long enough. And I had plenty of time. I'd be with Dad driving back from the nursing home, and the traffic was so heavy that it took several turns to get through the stoplight, more than enough time to look at a weedy lot. I'd think about the Shaw family. I wondered how they lived after that accident.

Three years after that awful June day, they bought a new split-level house in the next town, four miles from the Ferris wheel. To go west from their house, one would usually take Jericho Turnpike, but if they did, they would have to drive past the stalled Ferris wheel, unless they maneuvered to miss it forever, taking the parkway or expressway two or three exits west. But that would have meant a lifetime of circumnavigation, an act that would have magnified the tragedy, as if their loss had grown to occupy the entire landscape. If they planned their route to avoid it, that was an acknowledgment, allowing the Ferris wheel to grow in size until it blocked the way, ruling many square miles, and they were living in its shade wherever they went. And maybe they were.

But it's been years since I was back in the old neighborhood. After my parents died, we sold the family home. The last time I was at our house on "my street," I remembered where I was the moment that I was riding my bike without training wheels for the first time. Dad was holding the back of the seat after we left our driveway, holding me steady. Three houses down the street, I looked behind, and I was on my own.

PART IV

MOMENTS, NOT MONUMENTS.

How do you build a clock that will run by itself for ten thousand years?
THE LONG NOW FOUNDATION.

THE CLOCK OF NOW-NOW-NOW

In the desert of West Texas, inside a mountain, in a shaft bored five hundred feet deep, is a clock designed to count time for the next ten thousand years. Civilization has had, thus far, about a ten-thousand-year run. The conjurers of this clock want us to believe that another ten thousand years is possible. The clock is a technological sleight of hand, but even more so, it is a virtuoso act of optimism. Monuments usually look to the past; this clock looks to the future.

"We can do little good for our dead," says Stewart Brand; but we can, with each action, help people we will never meet. We can, he believes, shape the future. "The soon-to-be outnumber the living," he says, so the "living have a greater impact on the unborn than ever before." Brand, best known for his *Whole Earth Catalog*, is one of the founders of the Long Now Foundation, which is building the clock in the mountain, the Clock of the Long Now. The clock is a memorial to the future. It's meant to be a beacon, a place of contemplation and possibility, a breathing space.

This time-altering idea was born, in part, in the rough-shorn Manhattan of the 1970s when the city came close to bankruptcy (breeding the famous *Daily News* headline when President Gerald Ford refused to help: "Ford to City: Drop Dead"). The British musician and composer Brian Eno arrived in New York to produce the Talking Heads' second record. "Everything was exciting, fast, current, and temporary," Eno says.

> *Enormous buildings came and went; careers rose and crashed in weeks. You rarely got the feeling that anyone had the time to think*

> *two years ahead, let alone ten or a hundred. Everyone seemed to be passing through. It was undeniably lively, but the downside was that it seemed selfish, irresponsible and randomly dangerous. I came to think of this as "The Short Now," and this suggested the possibility of its opposite—"The Long Now."*
>
> *The longer your sense of now, the more past and future it includes. It's ironic that, at a time when humankind is at a peak of its technical powers, able to create huge global changes that will echo down the centuries, most of our social systems seem geared to increasingly short nows. Huge industries feel pressure to plan for the bottom line and the next shareholders meeting. Politicians feel forced to perform for the next election or opinion poll. The media attract bigger audiences by spurring instant and heated reactions to human interest stories while overlooking longer-term issues—the real human interest.*

The tempo has quickened since then; the 1970s seem like a quaint, analog relic. Our time horizon has shrunk; our power exceeds our vision. We live in a time of twitchy hustle tied to the Clock of Now-Now-Now.

Year by year, the Short Now has been tightening its grip on us. Cast your net into the water, and you'll come up with worry about the quickening pace of life, about "American Nervousness" as a popular book called it in 1881. Americans are uniquely nervous, said George Beard. "The Greeks were certainly civilized, but they were not nervous, and in the Greek language there is no word for that term." Another writer in 1901 diagnosed "American Nervousness" as "New Yorkitis." The noisy city "kept the nerves jangling day after day and night after night," said John H. Girdner. People were cut off from the real life of the farm and country, he said.

The steam engine had overturned centuries of animal strength and animal time. The horse had been the timekeeper; the horse had set the rhythm, had set the distance for a day's journey. The railroad and the telegraph replaced horses and accelerated life. The countryside passed by in a blur. "The speed is something unheard of. The flowers on the road are no longer flowers, but spots, or rather red or white stripes," said a disoriented Victor Hugo after riding the first passenger train in 1837. "The wheat is a big yellow blur. . . . Towns, steeples, and trees dance and mingle madly on the horizon." Hugo's train was racing along at about twenty-eight miles per hour, almost six times faster than a horse pulling a wagon.

Places that were once separated by days and weeks of hard travel were now only hours away. It's "as if the mountains and forests of all countries were advancing on Paris," said Heinrich Heine in the same era. The old measures of place and time were overthrown. The railroads created a new clock, carving the map into zones of time, replacing local time—each town and city had observed noon when the sun was at its highest. When it was noon in Chicago, it was 11:50 a.m. in St. Louis and 12:18 in Detroit. Local time was obsolete; your village, your few acres, were joined to the world. The railroad, this big machine, replaced "sun time."

Henry Adams, a historian attuned to the changing rhythms of the nineteenth century, took its measure:

> *The world did not double or treble its movement between 1800 and 1900, but, measured by any standard known to science—by horse-power, calories, volts, mass in any shape—the tension and vibration and volume and so-called progression of society were fully a thousand times greater in 1900 than in 1800—the force had doubled ten times over, and the speed, when measured by electrical standards as in telegraphy, approached infinity, and had annihilated both space and time.*

Space and time were annihilated; work and leisure changed. Entertainment changed. Vaudeville rode the rails to the smallest cities. Vaudeville was fast—the actor had to deliver an act in just fifteen or thirty minutes, to present in a sketch what had been previously spun out over three acts. "The effect must be vivid, instantaneous, and unmistakable," said a theater critic in 1914. Vaudeville actors moved to an urban, up-tempo time.

"All the old rhythm is gone and in its place is heard the hum of an engine, the whirr of wheels, the explosion of an exhaust," said the great songwriter Irving Berlin in 1924. "The leisurely songs that men hummed to the clatter of horses' hoofs do not fit into this new rhythm. . . . The new age demands new music for new action." And things have been accelerating ever since with "now" getting shorter and shorter. "Civilization," says Brand, "is revving itself into a pathologically short attention span." Let's rephrase Irving Berlin: The new age demands new monuments.

"The clock is a provocation," says Eno. It is a bid to put the brakes on the ever-narrowing now. It's trying to do this in a clever way, not by abandoning now, but by making it last ten thousand years. That's your new now. The Clock of the Long Now wants to redefine *now*, to elongate now even as we're drowning in now, in the rush of events and images. But can we elongate now, build a ladder out of the suffocating present, out of a time when vision narrows?

"Humanity has lots of artifacts that help us extend our imagination to the past," says Danny Hillis, a computer pioneer who first proposed the clock and has spent years designing it. He says,

> *The great pyramids are an example. You see a picture of a pyramid in the desert, and you naturally think about the people who built it. It conjures up a memory of the long human history that shaped our own culture. But we really don't have any such symbols for the future. What do we have that connects us to a thousand years ahead of us? Maybe science fiction, which helps us imagine specific hypothetical futures. The clock is more open-ended. It helps us imagine a future unconstrained by specific predictions. It gives us room to imagine. The ten-thousand-year time frame reminds us that our future is very big and so it's worth striving to make it better.*

Hillis doesn't see time as a predator. He's an optimist. If we extend the timeline, we can give ourselves a chance to do great things. "I know this is a controversial idea these days, but I believe that over the long view of history, people really are getting better," he says. "On a millennial timescale, we humans have been repeatedly expanding our circle of empathy. I believe that is what Martin Luther King was talking about when he said, 'The arc of the moral universe is long, but it bends toward justice.'"

The clock gives people permission to think long term. "I think of the oak beams in the ceiling of College Hall at New College, Oxford," he says.

> *Last century, when the beams needed replacing, carpenters used oak trees that had been planted in 1386 when the dining hall was first built. The fourteenth-century builder had planted the trees in anticipation of the time, hundreds of years in the future, when the beams would need replacing. Did the carpenters plant new trees to replace the beams again a few hundred years from now?*

"Over the long term, the future is decided by optimists," says Kevin Kelly, the cofounder of *Wired* magazine and a clock advocate. "Optimism enables us to reach good and great things beyond the capability of a single generation."

And yet we persist in planting stone in the ground, measuring one tick of the clock. Every monument says, this name, this memory, forever and ever. Each time we do that, it's as if we were riding a raft caught in a torrent, reaching out to grab anything to stop ourselves from being washed away.

The Clock of the Long Now makes explicit what is left unsaid—monuments are about time. Here is the last place that the Great One stood. This is when the clock stopped. This is about death. We must make death into a stone so we can believe it, so that we at last stand still long enough to admit it. We are all clocks ticking from the day we're born. Memorials and cemeteries are timepieces. Tick-tock, and tick-tock no more. But the clock isn't a tale of a completed life, a circuit of months and years. It wants to be an arrow shot toward the future, as if we could ride time's arrow forward to think of what's to come.

The clock is an attempt to plant the future in our view, to tie our days to the next day and the day after that. It aims to say, "This morning is the first day of the next ten thousand years." "Time is asymmetrical for us. We can see the past but not influence it," says Brand. "We can influence the future but not see it." This is a memorial to the unknown child who will be born in a year when we're no longer alive. The future may be our biggest invisible monument. The clock's acolytes hope that they can lead us to dream a new future.

Perhaps the strangest thing about the clock is that it is being built, helped along by $42 million from billionaire Jeff Bezos.

This is an improbable monument that none of us will probably ever visit, but the acolytes of the clock who have imagined this entire project want us to see what they see. "To see the clock you need to start at dawn, like any pilgrimage," says Kelly. It will be a trying journey, says Hillis.

> *At the start of the trail, you can see the site of the clock with a pair of binoculars from a far distance, but as you get closer, the route is designed so that it disappears from view. You would wonder constantly if you are lost and about to come to a dead end. You will need to squeeze through a narrow slot with sheer walls and then you have to climb up a cliff, using hanging chain ladders. When you finally arrive at the base of the mountain, you are confronted with this unclimbable five-hundred-foot cliff. There is a tiny entrance at the bottom of it that looks like an old mine entrance.*

Hillis, who spent time as a Disney Imagineer and has a profound love of play, sounds like he is describing a scene from *Raiders of the Lost Ark*:

> *Just inside there is a crank you can turn to give you a little bit of light. It illuminates a ladder that goes down into a natural cave. By now,*

> *you're probably wondering if you're in the right place. You wander through the natural cave formations until you find a tiny hole in the back of the cave that you can slip through. It takes you into a carved tunnel that leads you to the first thing that really feels like you're getting to the clock: a big metal door that hinges upward. The door opens an airlock to the clock. Once you go inside, there's another door behind it, and you'll discover that you can't open the next door until you drop and let it close. So there's a moment of truth. You have to close the first door to open the second. That marks the transition.*

The pilgrim has only now arrived at this technological temple deep in the mountain, one imbued with the slow-time hush of a medieval abbey. It is a shrine to the faith that a clever-enough machine can lift our vision. At a stainless-steel door, "you rotate its round handles to let yourself in and then seal the doors behind you," says Kelly.

> *It is totally black. You head into the darkness of a tunnel a few hundred feet long. At the end there's the mildest hint of light on the floor. You look up. There is a tiny dot of light far away, at the top of a five-hundred-foot-long vertical tunnel about twelve feet in diameter. The dot of light beckons you. You begin the ascent. You start climbing a continuous spiral staircase, winding up the outer rim of the tunnel, rising toward the very faint light overhead. The stairs are carved out of the rock.*

This is the work of a "special stone-slicing robot," which was invented to steadily grind out the precise steps.

Kelly continues,

> *Round the tunnel and up the tube toward the light you head. The first part of the clock you encounter on the ascent up the spiral staircase is the counterweights of the clock's drive system. This is a huge stack of stone disks, about the size of a small car and weighing ten thousand pounds. Depending on when the clock was last wound, you may have to climb seventy-five feet before you reach the weights. . . . It takes*

> *two or three visitors to push around the capstan of the clock and to lift its ten-thousand-pound stones. You rotate around until you can no further. Now the clock is wound.*
>
> *You keep climbing. For the next seventy to eighty feet of ascent, you pass twenty huge horizontal gears (called Geneva wheels), eight feet in diameter, each weighing one thousand pounds. This is the mechanical computer that calculates the over 3.5 million different melodies that the chimes will ring inside the mountain over the centuries. The chimes never repeat so that every visitor's experience is unique, and the calculated variety creates a sense of progressive time, rather than endless recycling.*

Brian Eno composed the music for the chimes.

Kelly concludes,

> *Finally, way out of breath, you arrive at the primary chamber. Here is the face of the clock. A disk about eight feet in diameter artfully displays the natural cycles of astronomical time, the pace of the stars and the planets, and the galactic time of the Earth's procession. If you peer deep into the clock's workings, you can also see the time of day. . . . To save energy, the clock will not move its dials unless they are turned, that is, powered, by a visitor. The clock calculates the correct time but will only display the correct time if you wind up its display wheel. So yet another hand-turned wheel awaits your effort to update the face of time.*

Hillis hopes that this journey "will help pilgrims feel the continuity, that great continuity, with our deep past and our long future. . . . You are having to leave behind the ordinary world and enter into a different one. One that will stretch your sense of time."

The pilgrims have walked clear of the haze of our daily hurry. They have been freed by contemplating the "world's slowest computer." The Clock of the Long Now is like a mechanical monk in a monastery, saving important knowledge from vanishing.

Some of Danny Hillis's old friends think the clock is a folly, a waste of his time and talent. "The way to make something last ten thousand years is to create an oral tradition. We don't need the clock so much as we need to start the myth of the clock," says one friend. But Hillis thinks that it is worth building the clock if he "can inspire 10 percent of the engineers in Silicon Valley to spend 10 percent of their time thinking about problems whose solution is more than ten years out into the future." He is a philosopher-engineer, says one magazine profile. His "inventions are meta technology—technology that has as its purpose changing the way we think about technology."

In one of his early designs, Hillis proposed that the clock be powered only by visitors: "If it's forgotten, it stops." This is true of many of our monuments. Our landscape is a jumble shop of forgotten memorials. They are stopped clocks, discarded clocks, invisible monuments. The monument that we need is one that proclaims, "Now-now-now." This is not the blazing moment, but a now of ten thousand years, a now of consequences and possibilities. Kelly makes the case for the clock by adopting a question from medical pioneer Jonas Salk: "Are we being good ancestors?" By thinking long-term, Kelly says, "we can become better ancestors."

There are plans for other Long Now clocks. The Smithsonian is interested in one. We could use the equivalent of the Monumental Bronze Company and its production of zinc Civil War statues. We need monuments, gestures, reminders about the future—and how the future lives *now*—in our every action. I wish there could be a Clock of the Long Now on town commons and Main Streets and in city parks to join the zinc Civil War soldiers, the rosters in bronze of the dead from the wars. A monument that would say, "The future starts now. This is the starting line." A monument that asks, "Are you being a good ancestor?"

Winter on the common of a small New Hampshire town. HOWARD MANSFIELD.

MOMENT-MOMENT-MOMENT

For the first artists in the early 1800s, the wilderness of New Hampshire's White Mountains was a place awaiting their discovery, a place they would conjure, moment by moment. Their great landscape paintings were encounters with a little holy terror. They implied that God was near. They were about a vast land, about wonder that bled off the canvas. The huge mountains suggested mountains without end. They suggested that greatness without end awaited the young nation.

The best of their landscape paintings are a call and response. When we see a moment of changing light, when the mountain itself seems to change as we look at it, time and again, that's what we're witnessing. It's just an old landscape painting in a fancy frame hanging on a wall, and yet it seems animated.

And this is why: The world is a call and response. We see the mountain, and in some sense that's crazy to say aloud, the mountain sees us. It doesn't say, *Have a nice day!* or *Hey! Lookin' good in those L.L. Bean Mt. Katahdin hiking shorts in slate gray.* But it says, in some way, *Of all the forms that I have been—twice as tall, eroded and risen again, drifted and collided, swept by glaciers and released—of all those forms, here I am.*

In that moment, there we are together; one person—one of billions who have ever lived—and a mountain, millions of years old. The continents drifted, the mountains rose up and up, were eroded, covered by ice, the ice receded. Forests grew tall, were clear cut, grew back. How extraordinary to be here together in this vast, expanding, ancient universe.

How extraordinary to be here in that moment. Blood and breath, granite and pine.

Call and response. And that happens moment by moment. The moment arises and passes. The next moment arises. For example, let's take the moment you met your spouse—though you may have dated for weeks, months, maybe longer—the true meeting happened in a moment. Teachers sometimes call it the "teachable moment"—the moment when, amid the class schedules, the bells and buses, and the entire to-and-fro of the day, the teacher and student at last connect. Or think of the moment in the interview when you won the job, the sale, the big prize. There was a lot of prologue, emails exchanged, proposals sent, arrangements to meet, chitchat about traffic and so on as you sat down, but the heart of the matter, the yes or no, happens in a moment. You connect, or you don't.

Moment-moment-moment. We are most alive moment by moment. We are most alive when we are partaking in the call and response of the world.

Those artists in the White Mountains saw the mountains in a moment. They set down something of the mountain's essence in a sketch, in brush strokes and colors. In that moment they were alive. That's why they had traveled for days, on foot, by horse, and later by train, camped out in rough boardinghouses and later better hotels. It's why they lugged their "trap"—easel, paints, and umbrella—out each day, often to the same spot day after day. They were making themselves ready for the moment when they'd be fully alive. *Call and response.*

The mountain rose up before them like a whale breaching, the sudden presence of a massive, breathing being—all sunlight and shadow, dark and light greens, elusive mottled grays—and in a moment, they saw it. First sight, fresh sight, insight.

"Crossing a bare common," Ralph Waldo Emerson writes in his essay *Nature*, "in snow puddles, at twilight, under a clouded sky, without having in my thoughts any occurrence of special good fortune, I have enjoyed a perfect exhilaration. I am glad to the brink of fear."

Emerson is not exalting in a view from the south rim of the Grand Canyon. He's not at the edge of a cliff where it falls into the Pacific surf at Big Sur, seeming to feel the continent falling into the sea. No. It's late on a winter's day when the snow is in slushy puddles. The trees bare; the ground a hardscrabble of ice and snow. This is not the photo for the December calendar page. It's one moment in the universe. That's what arises in us—the universe, the soul—call it what you will—moment by moment.

And here we are. As the Buddhists teach, the donkey sees the well, *and* the well sees the donkey. Mind creates the world. There is no division. Outside is inside. How glorious, how mysterious to be one person on one mountain in one moment.

Moment-moment-moment.

Moments, not monuments.

A hidden memorial, the fingerprints of the enslaved brickmaker in a brick found at Rose Hill Plantation, Union, South Carolina. NATHAN JOHNSON, ROSE HILL PLANTATION STATE HISTORIC SITE, SOUTH CAROLINA STATE PARKS.

CODA: THE FINGERPRINTS IN THE BRICK

At the Rose Hill Plantation in South Carolina, in the oddly named town of Union, is a small testament: one red brick with three deeply impressed fingerprints. They are the accidental mark of the enslaved brickmaker. This rough brick, still looking like clay, is a truth-telling monument, a hint for us to look further. Three fingertips, once part of a hand, a life, a soul, trapped in an economy built by forced labor. The plantation encompassed two thousand acres, where 178 other enslaved "hands" grew cotton and corn.

Rose Hill was the home of William Henry Gist, the "Secession Governor," in office from 1858 to 1860, who pushed for South Carolina to leave the Union. The Gist family lived well here. Striving for grandeur, Gist remodeled his house by adding a classical porch and stuccoing the exterior to create Rose Hill Mansion. That information is on the state's metal historical marker: "Its fanlights, carved doors and spiral staircase are noteworthy." Nothing is said about the enslaved labor to build and clean the house, cook the food, wash the family's clothes, and grow the crops. Most online sources follow the pattern, talking about the Gists, their mansion, and land and saying no more, willing the truth into invisibility.

Today forty-four acres of the plantation are a state park. Only the mansion, a kitchen house, and the ruins of postemancipation tenant farmers' houses are left. "The location of 'slave quarters' remains unknown," say the park rangers, "but we are searching for answers." The enslaved were housed in as many as twenty buildings. The Gist family cemetery, with fourteen graves, is one mile away, and buried nearby are their slaves in their own cemetery, in unmarked graves. The rangers are looking into that, too: "No sign has been erected at the cemetery, but the park is exploring options for providing accessibility and interpretation at the site."

And then there's that brick, and others, too, including one dug up from an old garden wall. "There aren't a lot of physical resources to connect us to enslaved people here. It's a way to put your finger in those fingerprints and feel connected," says Nate Johnson, the plantation's park manager. "These fingerprints are really all around us, here and at several other historic sites. But a lot of people just don't know about them."

One of the bricks they found at the plantation shows the path of a cat. "That brick has captured a bit of the human experience," Johnson says. "We see the moment a cat, or kitty, walked across the brick as it was in the mold, setting. You can almost picture that brick maker trying to shoo the cat away. It puts you in the moment."

These handmade bricks with fingerprints keep showing up across the South in chimneys, walls, and foundations, each brick a witness.

ACKNOWLEDGMENTS

FOR TAKING THE TIME TO VISIT THE IRISH, I THANK POET HENRY Walters and musician Steve Schuch. My thanks also to Henry for reviewing the chapter "When the War Between the Corkonians and Far Downs Came to America." Jim Garvin, New Hampshire's all-time master of state history, walked the Summit Cut with me, a tour that was invaluable.

A number of historians answered my questions and guided me to references. They have a vast understanding of railroads and how they changed America: Tom Berry, Brad Blodget, Richard White, and C. J. Schnexnayder.

For pitching in their expert knowledge of the local landscape, I thank anthropologist Robert Goodby, retired state archivist Brian Nelson Burford, Willard and Holly Williams for their equine expertise, and Duncan Watson for his knowledge about Keene's landfill.

Thanks also to Jim Walters for his information on the Parmele family and to the Doane Family Association for taking the time to research my question: Susie Fauteux, Janet Jeffries, Tom King, and Pat Wells.

Don Upton was a gracious host at the Cathedral of the Pines. Bill Sloane added his recollections. Suzanne M. Woodland, deputy city manager/regulatory counsel, City of Portsmouth, New Hampshire, patiently fielded many emails about the city's African Burial Ground. Retired Judge Phil Runyon assessed the fate of a key court case. Historian Kerby Miller fielded my questions about Irish immigration.

Thanks to Scott Mansfield for reading the chapter "Falling from a Ferris Wheel" and to Jane Eklund, Jim Garvin, and Brad Blodget for reading "When the War Between the Corkonians and Far Downs Came to America."

Once again, many thanks are due to ace librarian Amy Markus for finding a number of hard-to-get books and charming some reluctant institutions to send them along.

A version of "A Parade, a Picnic, a Revolution" appeared in *Yankee* magazine. My thanks to editor Mel Allen for suggesting the assignment at a time when I was thinking about monuments and to park ranger David Harrigan for his thoughtful interview. Thanks also to Liza Stearns, the director of visitor engagement, education, and the arts for the National Parks of Boston.

The quotations by Patrick Kavanagh are from *Collected Poems*, edited by Antoinette Quinn (Allen Lane, 2004), by kind permission of the Trustees of the Estate of the late Katherine B. Kavanagh, through the Jonathan Williams Literary Agency. "Facing It" is from *Pleasure Dome: New and Collected Poems*, © 2001 by Yusef Komunyakaa, published by Wesleyan University Press, used by permission.

As always, my deepest thanks to my wife and editor, the octopus whisperer, turtle wrangler, and caretaker of good creatures, Sy Montgomery.

BIBLIOGRAPHY

The Empty Tomb

Cenotaph

Aslet, Clive, and Jane Ridley. "Lutyens and the Cenotaph: Architecture of Profound Emotion." Moderated by Martin Lutyens and Robin Prater, November 12, 2020. Posted November 19, 2020, by Lutyens Trust America. YouTube. 51 mins., 34 secs. https://www.youtube.com/watch?v=Y8a0RETOFik.

Cannadine, David. "War and Death, Grief and Mourning in Modern Britain." In *Mirrors of Mortality: Studies in the Social History of Death*, edited by Joachim Whaley. St. Martin's Press, 1981.

Commonwealth War Graves Commission. "To Commemorate and Remember—Our Story." Accessed March 8, 2026. https://www.cwgc.org/who-we-are/our-story/.

Daily Herald. "England Honours Its Unknown Dead." November 12, 1920.

Daily Mail. "Army Spiritualists. Greeting the Dead. Sir A. Conan Doyle and the Scoffers." April 28, 1919.

Daily Mirror. "Night and Day Pilgrimage Past the Cenotaph." November 13, 1920.

Daily Mirror. "Wonderful Sunday Scenes at the Cenotaph." November 15, 1920.

Daily Telegraph. "Cenotaph Queue." November 12, 1920.

Daily Telegraph. "The Glorious Dead." July 18, 1919.

Daily Telegraph. "The Great Silence." November 12, 1920.

Daily Telegraph. "King and People at the Cenotaph." November 12, 1920.

Daily Telegraph. "Pilgrimage to the Cenotaph." November 13, 1920.

Dyer, Geoff. *The Missing of the Somme*. Vintage Books, 2011.

Evening Standard. "Children's Day at the Cenotaph." November 13, 1920.

Evening Standard. "To Their Immortal Memory." November 11, 1919.

Filler, Martin. "The Charms of Edwin Lutyens." *New York Review of Books*, December 4, 2014.

Foster, Ann-Marie. "The Bureaucratization of Death: The First World War, Families, and the State." *Twentieth Century British History* 33, no. 4 (December 2022).

Foster, Ann-Marie. "Commemoration, Cult of the Fallen (Great Britain and Ireland)." In *International Encyclopedia of the First World War*, edited by Ute Daniel, Peter Gatrell, Oliver Janz, et al. Freie Universität Berlin, updated August 5, 2020. https://encyclopedia.1914-1918-online.net/article/commemoration-cult-of-the-fallen-great-britain-and-ireland/.

Gedling, Jon, and Martin Lutyens. "Thiepval: The Memorial to the Missing of the Somme." Moderated by Robin Prater. Posted November 26, 2021, by Lutyens Trust America. YouTube. 59 mins., 12 secs. https://www.youtube.com/watch?v=tHps4MLeB3g.

Graphic. "The Great Silence in the Streets of London." November 15, 1919.

Graphic. "The Way of the World." November 20, 1920.

Greenberg, Allan. "Lutyens' Cenotaph." *Journal of the Society of Architectural Historians* 48, no. 1 (March 1989).

Gregory, Adrian. *The Silence of Memory: Armistice Day 1919–1946*. Berg, 1994.

Hussey, Christopher, and Edwin Landseer. *The Life of Sir Edwin Lutyens*. Antique Collectors' Club, 1984.

Hynes, Samuel. *A War Imagined: The First World War and English Culture*. Maxwell Macmillan International, 1991.

Imperial War Museums. "The Pals Battalions of the First World War." Accessed March 8, 2026. https://www.iwm.org.uk/history/the-pals-battalions-of-the-first-world-war.

Jalland, Patricia. "Bereavement and Mourning (Great Britain)." In *International Encyclopedia of the First World War*, edited by Ute Daniel,

Peter Gatrell, Oliver Janz, et al. Freie Universität Berlin, updated October 8, 2014. https://encyclopedia.1914-1918-online.net/article/bereavement-and-mourning-great-britain/.

Jeffrey, Keith. *1916: A Global History*. Bloomsbury, 2016.

Keegan, John. *The First World War*. Alfred A. Knopf, 1999.

Kenyon, Frederic. *War Graves: How the Cemeteries Abroad Will Be Designed*. Report to the Imperial War Graves Commission. His Majesty's Stationery Office, 1918.

Kipling, Rudyard. *The Graves of the Fallen*. Imperial War Graves Commission, 1919.

Manchester Guardian. "The Cenotaph and the Cross." July 29, 1919.

Moffett, Alex. "'We Will Remember Them': The Poetic Rewritings of Lutyens' Cenotaph." *War Literature and the Arts: An Interdisciplinary Journal* 19, nos. 1–2 (2007).

The People. "Tribute to the Mighty Dead." November 16, 1919.

Scully, Vincent. "The Terrible Art of Designing a War Memorial." *New York Times*, July 14, 1991.

Stamp, Gavin. *The Memorial to the Missing of the Somme*. Profile Books, 2010.

Stavely-Wadham, Rose. "Understanding the 1920s Spiritualism Revival." *British Newspaper Archive* (blog). October 14, 2021. https://blog.britishnewspaperarchive.co.uk/2021/10/14/understanding-the-1920s-spiritualism-revival/.

Times of London. "Armistice Day, 1920."

Times of London. "The Art of the Cenotaph." November 11, 1920.

Times of London. "At the Cenotaph." July 21, 1919.

Times of London. "Before the Cenotaph." November 12, 1919.

Times of London. "Call of the Cenotaph." November 15, 1920.

Times of London. "The Great Pilgrimage." November 12, 1920.

Times of London. "The People's Homage." November 13, 1920.

Tison, Stéphane. "Commemoration, Cult of the Fallen." In *International Encyclopedia of the First World War*, edited by Ute Daniel, Peter Gatrell, Oliver Janz, et al. Freie Universität Berlin, updated February 11, 2019. https://encyclopedia.1914-1918-online.net/article/commemoration-cult-of-the-fallen/.

Weekly Dispatch. "The Day's Dramatic Moment." July 20, 1919.
Weekly Dispatch. "The Nation Passing Down Whitehall." November 14, 1920.
Whitmore, Lucie. "'A Matter of Individual Opinion and Feeling': The Changing Culture of Mourning Dress in the First World War." *Women's History Review* 27, no. 4 (2018).
Winter, Jay. *Sites of Memory, Sites of Mourning: The Great War in European Cultural History*. Cambridge University Press, 1995.

Vietnam Veterans Memorial

Abramson, Daniel. "Maya Lin and the 1960s: Monuments, Time Lines, and Minimalism." *Critical Inquiry* 22, no. 4 (Summer 1996).
Andersen, Kurt. "American Icons: The Vietnam Veterans Memorial." Studio360. October 4, 2013. https://www.wnyc.org/story/american-icons-the-vietnam-veterans-memorial.
Hass, Kristin Ann. *Carried to the Wall: American Memory and the Vietnam Veterans Memorial*. University of California Press, 1998.
Komunyakaa, Yusef. *Pleasure Dome: New and Collected Poems*. Wesleyan University Press, 2001.
Lin, Maya. *Boundaries*. Simon & Schuster, 2000.
Lin, Maya. *Systematic Landscapes*. Yale University Press, 2006.
Menand, Louis. "Maya Lin, the Reluctant Memorialist." *New Yorker*, June 30, 2002.
Nguyen, Viet Thanh. "Nothing Ever Dies: Vietnam and the Memory of War." Interview by Michael Vann. May 29, 2020. https://vietnguyen.info/2020/viet-thanh-nguyen-nothing-ever-dies-vietnam-and-the-memory-of-war.
Nguyen, Viet Thanh. *Nothing Ever Dies: Vietnam and the Memory of War*. Harvard University Press, 2016.
Nguyen, Viet Thanh. "Our Vietnam War Never Ended." *New York Times*, April 24, 2015.
Nguyen, Viet Thanh. "War, Memory and the Future." *Asian American Literary Review* 2, no. 1 (Winter/Spring 2011).
Palmer, Laura. *Shrapnel in the Heart*. Random House, 1987.

Savage, Kirk. *Monument Wars: Washington, D.C., the National Mall, and the Transformation of the Memorial Landscape.* University of California Press, 2009.

Tauber, Peter. "Monument Maker." *New York Times Magazine*, February 24, 1991.

Vietnam Veterans Memorial Fund. "Wall Audit Summary." May 23, 2019. https://www.vvmf.org/News/wall-audit-completed/.

Jochen Gerz

"2146 Stones—Monument Against Racism." CIPDH International Center for the Promotion of Human Rights. 2019. www.cipdh.gob.ar/memorias-situadas/en/lugar-de-memoria/2146-piedras-monumento-contra-el-racismo/.

Callaghan, Mark. "Invisible Past, Invisible Future: A German's Alternative Response to the Holocaust." *Art Times*, November/December 2010.

Eichler, Jeremy. *Time's Echo: The Second World War, the Holocaust, and the Music of Remembrance.* Alfred A. Knopf, 2023.

"Invisible Memorial Square." Information Portal to European Sites of Remembrance Staettens. Accessed April 1, 2026. https://www.memorialmuseums.org/.

Mansfield, Howard. "Invisible Memorials and the Presence of Absence." *Washington Post*, May 23, 2024.

"Monument Against Fascism—Counter Monument." Accessed April 1, 2026. https://jochengerz.eu/works/monument-against-fascism.

Nielsen, Gustavo. "Jochen Gerz, el Artista de los Monumentos a la Memoria." ARQA. November 12, 2008. https://arqa.com/actualidad/colaboraciones/jochen-gerz-el-artista-de-los-monumentos-a-la-memoria.html.

Stevens, Quentin, Karen A. Franck, and Ruth Fazakerley. "Counter-Monuments: The Anti-Monumental and the Dialogic." *Journal of Architecture* 23, no. 5 (2018).

Young, James E. "The Counter-Monument: Memory Against Itself in Germany Today." *Critical Inquiry* (Winter 1992).

Young, James E. "Germany's Vanishing Holocaust Monuments." *Judaism: A Quarterly Journal of Jewish Life and Thought* (September 1994).
Young, James E. *The Texture of Memory: Holocaust Memorials and Meaning*. Yale University Press, 1993.

Other Monuments

Allen, Chadwick. "Performing Serpent Mound: A Trans-Indigenous Meditation." *Theatre Journal* 67, no. 3 (October 2015).
American Battle Monuments Commission. *Florence American Cemetery and Memorial.* American Battle Monuments Commission, n.d.
Austermuhle, Martin. "With Change Afoot, Skateboarders Rally to Preserve Freedom Plaza." DCist. March 31, 2022. https://dcist.com/story/22/03/31/freedom-plaza-skateboarders/.
Bailey, Spencer. *In Memory Of: Designing Contemporary Memorials.* Phaidon Press, 2020.
Beetham, Sarah. "'An Army of Bronze Simulacra': The Copied Soldier Monument and the American Civil War." n.d.
Bodnar, John. *The "Good War" in American Memory.* Johns Hopkins University Press, 2010.
Catalogue of the Monumental Bronze Co. Bridgeport, CT, October 1882.
Doss, Erika. *Memorial Mania: Public Feeling in America.* University of Chicago, 2010.
Eliade, Mircea. *The Sacred and the Profane*. Harcourt, Brace, 1959.
Fisher, Marc. "Why Those Confederate Soldier Statues Look a Lot Like Their Union Counterparts." *Washington Post*, August 18, 2017.
Foote, Kenneth E. *Shadowed Ground: America's Landscapes of Violence and Tragedy.* University of Texas Press, 1997.
Grissom, Carol A. *Zinc Sculpture in America, 1850–1950.* University of Delaware Press, 2009.
Grissom, Carol A., and Ronald S. Harvey. "The Conservation of American War Memorials Made of Zinc." *Journal of the American Institute for Conservation* 42, no. 1 (Spring 2003).
Howells, William Dean. "Question of Monuments." *Atlantic Monthly*, May 1866.

Ivanoff, Carolyn. "Monuments Everlasting—Bridgeport's Monumental Bronze Company." Bridgeport History Center Grassroots Historians Series, December 2019. https://bportlibrary.org/hc/business-and-commerce/monuments-everlasting-bridgeports-monumental-bronze-company/?utm_source=chatgpt.com.

Kimmelman, Michael. "Out of Minimalism, Monuments to Memory." *New York Times*, January 13, 2002.

Lichtenstein, Andrew, and Alex Lichtenstein. *Marked, Unmarked, Remembered: A Geography of American Memory*. West Virginia University Press, 2017.

Linenthal, Edward Tabor. *Sacred Ground: Americans and Their Battlefields*. University of Illinois Press, 1991.

Mansfield, Howard. "The Grief Police." In *The Bones of the Earth*. Shoemaker & Hoard, 2004.

Mumford, Lewis. *The Culture of Cities*. Harcourt, Brace, 1938.

Musil, Robert. *Selected Writings*. Continuum, 1986.

Musil, Robert, and Peter Wortsman, eds. *Posthumous Papers of a Living Author*. Eridanos Press, 1987.

Naughton, Jim. "The Battle of Bedford." *Washington Post*, May 24, 2003.

Rabinowitz, Mark, and Carol Grissom. "Conservation of American Zinc Sculpture: History of the Use of the Material and Case Studies of Treatment." In *Metal a ciel ouvert: La sculpture metallique d'exterieur du XIXe siecle au debut du XXe siècle [Identification, Conservation, Restoration—Open Air Metal: Outdoor Metallic Sculpture for the 19th to the Early 20th Century]*. SFIIC, 2014.

Reston, James. "The Monument Glut." *New York Times*, September 10, 1995.

Smith, Clint. "Monuments to the Unthinkable." *Atlantic*, December 2022.

A Parade, a Picnic, a Revolution

Adams, Abigail. Letter from Abigail Adams to John Adams, 18–20 June 1775. https://www.masshist.org/digitaladams/archive/doc?id=L17750618aa.

Bluestone, Daniel. *Buildings, Landscapes, and Memory*. Norton, 2011.

Bodnar, John. *Remaking America Public Memory, Commemoration, and Patriotism in the Twentieth Century*. Princeton University Press, 1994.

Greenough, Henry. *Form and Function: Remarks on Art, Design, and Architecture*. University of California Press, 1958.

Greenough, Henry. *Letters of Horatio Greenough to His Brother, Henry Greenough*. Ticknor, 1887.

Hannigan, David. "Battle of Bunker Hill Timeline." n.d.

Hannigan, David. Interview with the author, June 16, 2024.

Idzerda, Stanley J., Anne C. Loveland, and Marc H. Miller. *Lafayette, Hero of Two Worlds: The Art and Pageantry of His Farewell Tour of America, 1824–1825*. Queens Museum, 1989.

Massachusetts Historical Society. "The Decisive Day Is Come: The Battle of Bunker Hill." Accessed March 8, 2026. https://www.masshist.org/features/bunker-hill.

National Park Service. "The Battle of Bunker Hill (U.S. National Park Service)." Updated January 12, 2026. https://home.nps.gov/articles/000/the-battle-of-bunker-hill.htm?utm_source=chatgpt.com.

National Park Service. "Building the Bunker Hill Monument." https://www.nps.gov/articles/000/building-the-bunker-hill-monument.htm.

National Park Service. "Bunker Hill: Construction of the Monument." Updated January 12, 2026. https://www.nps.gov/articles/000/bunker-hill-construction-of-the-monument.htm.

National Park Service. "Bunker Hill: Living Memories." Updated January 12, 2026. https://www.nps.gov/articles/000/bunker-hill-living-memories.htm.

National Park Service. "Bunker Hill Memory." Updated January 8, 2025. https://www.nps.gov/articles/000/bunker-hill-memory.htm.

National Park Service. "Caleb Stark." Updated February 26, 2025. https://www.nps.gov/people/caleb-stark.htm.

National Park Service. "Lieutenant John Waller." Updated March 1, 2023. https://www.nps.gov/people/john-waller.htm.

National Park Service. "Remembering Revolution: Bunker Hill Monument." Updated January 2, 2025. https://www.nps.gov/bost/

remembering-revolution.htm#27EBF851-37AB-4F4E-AA50-9BEDD914F0CC.

National Park Service. "Revolutionary War Veteran and Widow Pensions." Updated August 8, 2023. https://www.nps.gov/articles/000/revolutionary-war-veteran-and-widow-pensions.htm.

Purcell, Sarah J. *Sealed with Blood: War, Sacrifice, and Memory in Revolutionary America.* University of Pennsylvania Press, 2002.

Rosiecki, Casimer. "Fields of Deception—the Bunker Hill Battlefield." National Park Service. Updated October 7, 2020. https://www.nps.gov/articles/bunker-hill-battlefield.htm.

Tuckerman, Henry T. *A Memorial of Horatio Greenough, Consisting of a Memoir, Selections from His Writings, and Tributes to His Genius.* G. P. Putnam, 1853.

Webster, Daniel. Dedication speech for the unveiling of the Bunker Hill Monument, June 17, 1843. American Battlefield Trust. https://www.battlefields.org/learn/primary-sources/dedication-speech-unveiling-bunker-hill-monument.

Webster, Daniel. *Webster's Address Delivered at the Completion of the Bunker Hill Monument, June 17, 1843.* Tappan and Dennet, 1843.

Wheildon, William W. *Memoir of Solomon Willard.* Monument Association, 1865.

Willard, Solomon. *Plans and Sections of the Obelisk on Bunker's Hill.* S. N. Dickinson, 1843.

Wright, Nathalia. *Horatio Greenough: The First American Sculptor.* University of Pennsylvania Press, 2016.

Walking on the Dead

Webster, Donovan, *Aftermath: The Remnants of War.* Pantheon Books, 1996.

New York

Berlin, Ira. *Many Thousands Gone: The First Two Centuries of Slavery in North America.* Belknap Press of Harvard University Press, 1998.

Berlin, Ira, and Leslie M. Harris, eds. *Slavery in New York.* New Press, 2005.

Bible Gateway. Accessed March 8, 2026. https://www.biblegateway.com.

Blakey, Michael L. "African Burial Ground Project: Paradigm for Cooperation?" *Museum International* 62, nos. 1–2 (2010). https://doi.org/10.1111/j.1468-0033.2010.01716.x.

Blakey, Michael L. "The New York African Burial Ground Phenomenon." *Southern Anthropologist* 22, no. 3 (1995). https://egrove.olemiss.edu/southern_anthropologist/vol22/iss3/4.

Blakey, Michael L., and Lesley M. Rankin-Hill, eds. *The Skeletal Biology of the New York African Burial Ground: Part 1.* Howard University Press, 2009. https://scholarworks.wm.edu/asbook/44.

Burrows, Edwin G., and Mike Wallace. *Gotham: A History of New York City to 1898.* Oxford University Press, 1999.

Cantwell, Anne-Marie, and Diana diZerega Wall. *Unearthing Gotham: The Archaeology of New York City.* Yale University Press, 2001.

Chan, Sewell. "Coffin's Emblem Defies Certainty." *New York Times*, January 26, 2010.

Dunlap, David W. "Dig Unearths Early Black Burial Ground." *New York Times*, October 9, 1991.

Frohne, Andrea E. *The African Burial Ground in New York City: Memory, Spirituality, and Space*. Syracuse University Press, 2015.

Harrington, Spencer P. M. "Bones and Bureaucrats: New York's Great Cemetery Imbroglio." *Archaeology*, March/April 1993. https://archive.archaeology.org/online/features/afrburial/.

Herndon, Lisa. "Reflection and Remembrance: The African Burial Ground, 30 Years After Discovery." New York Public Library. October 4, 2021.

Howson, Jean, Gale Harris, and Leonard G. Bianchi, et al. *New York African Burial Ground Archaeology Final Report*. Vol. 1. Howard University, 2006.

Howson, Jean, Gale Harris, and Betty Bradley. "African Burial Ground: National Register of Historic Places Registration Form." Department of the Interior, National Park Service, November 9, 1992.

Kearse, Bettye. "I Feared My Enslaved Ancestors Had Been Dishonored in Death—But the African Burial Ground in New York City Tells a Different Story." *Time*, March 24, 2020.

Kilgannon, Corey. "Public Lives: Unearthing the Past, Then Burying It with Respect." *New York Times*, October 2, 2003.

Kutz, David, dir. *The African Burial Ground: An American Discovery*. Kutz Television, 1994.

Medford, Edna Greene, ed. *Historical Perspectives of the African Burial Ground New York Blacks and the Diaspora*. Howard University Press, 2009. https://scholarworks.wm.edu/asbook/48.

Medford, Edna Greene, ed. *New York African Burial Ground History Final Report*. Howard University, 2004. https://core.tdar.org/document/4868/new-york-african-burial-ground-historyfinal-report.

National Park Service. *African Burial Ground National Monument*. Government Printing Office, 2011.

New-York Historical Society. "Buried Stories Lessons from the African Burial Ground." n.d. https://www.slaveryinnewyork.org/PDFs/Buried_Stories.pdf.

New York Preservation Archive Project. "African Burial Ground." N.d. https://www.nypap.org/preservation-history/african-burialground/.

Pedrick, Alexis, host. "The African Burial Ground." *Distillations*. Podcast. WFGD Studio, 2023.

Perry, Warren R. "The African Burial Ground: Legacy of Struggle." *Our Time Press*, December 2003. https://ourtimepress.com/the-african-burial-ground-legacy-of-struggle/?utm_source=chatgpt.com.

Perry, Warren R., Jean Howson, and Barbara A. Bianco, eds. *The Archaeology of the New York African Burial Ground: Part 1*. Howard University Press, 2009. https://scholarworks.wm.edu/asbook/45.

"Reburial for 400 Africans Is Commemorated in Six Cities." *Our Time Press*, October 2003. https://ourtimepress.com/reburial-for-400-africans-is-commemorated-in-six-cities/?utm_source=chatgpt.com.

Ross, Marc Howard. *Slavery in the North: Forgetting History and Recovering Memory*. University of Pennsylvania Press, 2018.

U.S. Congress. Pub. L. No. 102-393. 102nd Cong., 2nd Sess.. October 6, 1992.

Portsmouth

Blue Ribbon Committee on African Burial Ground. "African Burying Ground Project Timeline 2003–2010."

Blue Ribbon Committee on African Burial Ground. Meeting minutes, April 18, 2007; May 9, 2007; May 29, 2007; June 27, 2007; July 24, 2008; February 10, 2009; October 22, 2014.

Blue Ribbon Committee on African Burial Ground. Overview and Status. December 21, 2010.

Hall, Beth LaMontagne. "No Longer Forgotten: Portsmouth's African Burial Ground Memorial Park Prepares to Open." Seacoastonline.com, May 20, 2015.

Independent Archaeological Consulting. "Portsmouth African Burying Ground." June 15, 2018. https://www.iac-llc.net/project/portsmouth-african-burying-ground/.

Kenny, Elizabeth. "African American Memorial Discussed." *Portsmouth Herald*, May 6, 2007.

Leech, Adam. "Sides Taken on Burial Ground." *Portsmouth Herald*, November 18, 2008.

McDermott, Deborah. "African Burying Ground Construction Involves Careful Consideration." *Portsmouth Herald*, August 19, 2014.

McDermott, Deborah. "Challenges, Rewards of Creating a Legacy Park." *Fosters Daily Democrat*, May 10, 2015.

McDermott, Deborah. "A Monument to Community, Past and Present." *Seacoast Sunday*, May 22, 2011.

Parr, Jessica. "On Remembrance and Resurrection: Commemorating Portsmouth's (NH) African Burial Ground." *Junto* (blog). June 1, 2015. https://earlyamericanists.com/2015/06/01/on-remembrance-and-resurrection-commemorating-portsmouths-nh-african-burying-ground/?utm_source=chatgpt.com.

"Please Join Us as We Stand in Honor of Those Forgotten. May 20–23, 2015. Vigil Reburial Celebration." Portsmouth New Hampshire African Burying Ground.

Portsmouth African Burial Ground. "In Honor of Those Forgotten." October 2015. http://www.africanburyinggroundnh.org/.

"Portsmouth African Burying Ground: Rediscovery to Memorial." Portsmouth Athenaeum, Portsmouth, N.H., n.d.

Portsmouth, New Hampshire. "4.21.2025 African Burying Ground Stewardship Committee." Posted April 21, 2025, by City of Portsmouth, New Hampshire. YouTube. 38 min., 11 sec. https://www.youtube.com/watch?v=_CD6jG5ljNQ.

Portsmouth, New Hampshire. "City of Portsmouth Announces African Burying Ground Construction Start and Consecration Ceremony." August 15, 2014.

Portsmouth, New Hampshire. "Reburial Ceremony at African Burying Ground, Portsmouth, NH." Posted May 26, 2015, by City of Portsmouth, New Hampshire. YouTube. 2 hr., 25 min., 7 sec. https://www.youtube.com/watch?v=kPN_NBWI1I0&utm.

Public Art Review Committee. "Public Art in Portsmouth, NH, Inventory as of February 9, 2025." https://www.portsmouthnh.gov/sites/default/files/2025-02/PARC%20Art%20guide%20STS%20rev%20020925.pdf.

Robinson, J. Dennis. "Changing the Meaning of Space." TMS Architects Interiors. August 18, 2015. https://www.tmsarchitects.com/changing-the-meaning-of-space/.

Robinson, J. Dennis. "Portsmouth African Burial Ground Blues." Seacoastonline.com. 2007.

Sammons, Mark J., and Valerie Cunningham. *Black Portsmouth: Three Centuries of African-American Heritage.* University of New Hampshire Press, 2004.

Stevens, J. L. "Portsmouth Builds Memorial in Honor of Those Forgotten Twelve Years in the Making, the African Burying Ground Memorial in Portsmouth Brings a Community's Vision to Life." *Square*, May 7, 2015.

Vawter, Brian, dir. *Shadows Fall North.* University of New Hampshire's Center for the Humanities, in collaboration with Atlantic Media Productions, 2016.

Wheeler, Kathleen. *Addendum No.1: Archaeological Excavations at the Portsmouth African Burial Ground (27-Rk-384) Chestnut and Courts Streets Portsmouth (Rockingham County), New Hampshire. Results of*

November 2008 Archaeological Excavation. Independent Archaeological Consulting, final report, November 30, 2009.
Woodburn and Company Landscape Architecture. African Burial Ground public forum. Meeting notes, May 5, 2007.
Woodburn and Company Landscape Architecture. African Burial Ground public forum. Meeting notes, June 19, 2007.
Woodburn and Company Landscape Architecture. Sketches of five options, presented at African Burial Ground public forum, June 19, 2007.

Tampa
Baker Barrios Architects and Property Markets Group. *Zion Cemetery Memorial Plan: Research Phase Report.* Prepared for the Tampa Housing Authority. November 2020.
Drouzas, Frank. "Oral Histories of Erased Black Cemeteries: Yvette Lewis." *Weekly Challenger*, March 25, 2023.
George, Elizabeth, and Ian Hodgson. "Tampa's Oldest Public Housing Is Set to Be Demolished. Residents Celebrate History." *Tampa Bay Times*, August 28, 2024.
Guzzo, Paul. "10 Important Moments in the Story of Tampa's Erased Zion Cemetery." *Tampa Bay Times*, June 23, 2020.
Guzzo, Paul. "A Community, Not Just Zion Cemetery, Disappeared to Build Homes for Whites." *Tampa Bay Times*, November 4, 2019.
Guzzo, Paul. "A Complete Timeline of Tampa's Erased Zion Cemetery." *Tampa Bay Times*, August 26, 2020.
Guzzo, Paul. "The Lost Clearwater Heights Black Cemetery Might Be Under a Building." *Tampa Bay Times*, January 28, 2020.
Guzzo, Paul. "NAACP Wants Reparations for Tampa's Black Cemeteries That Governments 'Stole.'" *Tampa Bay Times*, February 27, 2023.
Guzzo, Paul. "Nearly 400 People Buried in Tampa Are Missing. What Happened to Zion Cemetery?" *Tampa Bay Times*, June 23, 2020.
Guzzo, Paul. "Radar Finds More than 120 Coffins Buried Beneath Tampa Apartment Complex." *Tampa Bay Times*, August 30, 2019.
Guzzo, Paul. "Search for Story of Zion Cemetery Shifts from Graves to Family Records." *Tampa Bay Times*, September 30, 2019.

Guzzo, Paul. "Who's Accountable for the Tragedy of Zion Cemetery? Chasing a Century-Old Mystery." *Tampa Bay Times*, September 6, 2019.

Guzzo, Paul, and Brandon Meyer. "In Search of Lost Cemeteries." *Tampa Bay Times*, December 30, 2019.

Historical Marker Database. "Zion Cemetery." Accessed March 8, 2026. https://www.hmdb.org/m.asp?m=267769.

Schreiner, Mark. "Zion Cemetery: What's Happened So Far and What's Next." WUSF. October 16, 2019.

Tampa, Florida. "Zion Cemetery Historical Marker Dedication Day." Proclamation, February 26, 2025.

Arlington

Arlington National Cemetery. *The Freedpeople of Section 27*. History Education Series. 2019.

Dennee, Timothy. "African-American Civilians Interred in Section 27 of Arlington National Cemetery, 1865–1867." Paper presented at 38th annual conference on D.C. Historical Studies, Goethe-Institut and the Martin Luther King Jr. Memorial Library, Washington, DC, November 3–6, 2011. https://38thdcstudiesconference.files.wordpress.com/2011/11/arlington-section27.pdf.

Fellman, Michael. *The Making of Robert E. Lee.* Random House, 2000.

McElya, Micki. *The Politics of Mourning: Death and Honor in Arlington National Cemetery*. Harvard University Press, 2016.

National Park Service. *Cultural Landscapes Inventory: Arlington House, the Robert E. Lee Memorial*. 2009.

Poole, Robert M. *On Hallowed Ground: The Story of Arlington National Cemetery.* Walker, 2009.

Other Burial Grounds

"Call to Artists/Request for Qualifications (RFQ) Bethel Burying Ground Memorial Project at Weccacoe Playground. Deadline for Submissions: December 30, 2019." City of Philadelphia. https://www.phila.gov/media/20200703181308/Bethel-Memorial-RFQ020191112.pdf.

Greco, JoAnn. "The Layered History of a Queen Village Site Newly Listed on the Register of Historic Place." Weitzman School of Design, University of Pennsylvania. October 10, 2016. https://www.design.upenn.edu/historic-preservation/post/penndesign%E2%80%99s-aaron-wunch-secures-successful-national-register-nomination.

Guillaume. "Remembering Those Buried at Bethel." *South Philly Review*, November 6, 2023.

Hill, Michael. "In Upstate New York, a Cemetery for People Who Were Enslaved Is Reclaimed." PBS News. August 30, 2024. https://www.pbs.org/newshour/nation/in-upstate-new-york-a-cemetery-for-people-who-were-enslaved-is-reclaimed.

Laterman, Kaye. "This Empty Lot Is Worth Millions. It's Also an African-American Burial Ground." *New York Times*, June 14, 2019.

Lauria, Maddy. "Unmarked Graves of Early Settlers, Slaves Found in Delaware." WVEC. December 6, 2017. https://www.13newsnow.com/article/news/history/unmarked-graves-of-early-settlers-slaves-found-in-delaware/291-497281522.

Lepore, Jill. "American Chronicles: The Underworld." *New Yorker*, October 4, 2021.

Menkevich, Joseph. Burial ground, Campbell A.M.E. Church of Frankford. "This nomination proposes to designate the burial ground and site at 1651 Kinsey Street as historic and list it on the Philadelphia Register of Historic Places." November 19, 2021.

New York Times. "Opinion: Documenting 'Slavery by Another Name' in Texas." Editorial. August 13, 2018.

North Carolina State Historic Preservation Office. Westview Cemetery, Wadesboro, North Carolina. National Register of Historic Places Registration Form, January 1, 2015.

Philadelphia, Office of Arts, Culture and the Creative Economy. Bethel Burying Ground Historic Site Memorial Committee. Call to Artists/Request for Qualifications (RFQ). Report.

Russ, Valerie. "City Celebrates New Plans for Bethel Burying Ground Art Memorial at Weccacoe Playground." *Philadelphia Inquirer*, November 7, 2023.

Sackman, Meghan. "Local Group Seeks to Landmark Elmhurst African Burial Ground, Protect from Development." *Jackson Heights Post*, November 12, 2018.

Shaw, Gwyneth K. "Testing Finds Signs of African-American Burial Ground Beneath Chestnut Street Property." *Penn Today*, February 7, 2019. https://penntoday.upenn.edu/news/testing-finds-signs-african-american-burial-ground-beneath-chestnut-street-property.

Smith, Ryan K. "Reclaiming Black History by Saving Black Cemeteries." *Time*, November 17, 2020.

Spikol, Liz. "Queen Village Neighbors vs. Friends of Bethel Burying Ground." *Philadelphia Magazine*, May 5, 2014.

Task Force on Abandoned African-American Cemeteries. Final report, Florida, December 17, 2021.

When the War Between the Corkonians and Far Downs Came to America

Ireland

Beames, M. R. "The Ribbon Societies: Lower-Class Nationalism in Pre-Famine Ireland." *Past & Present*, November 1982.

Beames, M. R. "Rural Conflict in Pre-Famine Ireland: Peasant Assassinations in Tipperary 1837–1847." *Past & Present*, November 1978.

Broeker, Galen. *Rural Disorder and Police Reform in Ireland, 1812–36*. Routledge & Kegan Paul, 1970.

Carson, Ciaran. *Last Night's Fun: In and Out of Time with Irish Music*. North Point Press, 1996.

Clark, Samuel, and James S. Donnelly Jr., eds. *Irish Peasants: Violence and Political Unrest 1780–1914*. University of Wisconsin Press, 2003.

Conley, Carolyn. "The Agreeable Recreation of Fighting." *Journal of Social History* (Autumn 1999).

Donnelly, James S., Jr. *The Land and the People of Nineteenth Century Cork*. Routledge & Kegan Paul, 1975.

Drudy, P. J., ed. *Ireland: Land, Politics and People*. Cambridge University Press, 1982.

Dunn, Mary Lee. *Ballykilcline Rising: From Famine Ireland to Immigrant America*. University of Massachusetts Press, 2008.

Garvin, Tom. "Defenders, Ribbonmen and Others: Underground Political Networks in Pre-Famine Ireland." *Past & Present*, August 1982.

Glassie, Henry. *Passing the Time in Ballymenone: Culture and History of an Ulster Community*. Indiana University Press, 1982.

Hoppen, K. Theodore. *Elections, Politics, and Society in Ireland 1832–1885.* Oxford University Press, 1984.

Huggins, Michael. *Social Conflict in Pre-Famine Ireland: The Case of County Roscommon.* Four Courts Press, 2007.

Hughes, Kyle, and Donald M. MacRaild, eds. *Crime, Violence, and the Irish in the 19th Century.* Liverpool University Press, 2017.

Hughes, Kyle, and Donald M. MacRaild. *Ribbon Societies in Nineteenth-Century Ireland and Its Diaspora.* Oxford University Press, 2018.

Joyce, Patrick. *Remembering Peasants: A Personal History of a Vanished World.* Scribner, 2024.

Lewis, George Cornewall. *On Local Disturbances in Ireland: And on the Irish Church Question.* B. Fellowes, 1836.

Macdonald, Fergus. *The Catholic Church and the Secret Societies in the United States.* United States Catholic Historical Society, c. 1946.

MacKillop, James. *A Dictionary of Celtic Mythology*. Oxford University Press, 2004.

Miller, Kerby A. *Emigrants and Exiles: Ireland and the Irish Exodus to North America.* Oxford University Press, 1985.

Moraghan, Sean. *Days of the Blackthorn: Faction Fighters of Kerry*. Mercier Press, 2020.

Norman, Edward. *A History of Modern Ireland.* Allen Lane, Penguin Press, 1971.

O'Donnell, Patrick. *The Irish Faction Fighters of the 19th Century*. Anvil Books, 1975.

O'Farrell, Patrick. *England and Ireland Since 1800.* Oxford University Press, 1975.

O'Tuathaigh, Gearoid. *Ireland Before the Famine 1798–1848.* Gill and Macmillan, 1972.

Scally, Robert James. *The End of Hidden Ireland: Rebellion, Famine, and Emigration*. Oxford University Press, 1995.

Williams, T. Desmond, ed. *Secret Societies in Ireland.* Gill and Macmillan, 1973.

Irish in America

Benes, Peter, ed. *The Irish in New England.* Dublin Seminar for New England Folklife, c. 2016.
Boston Pilot. Ads searching for lost family. July 10, 1847.
Boston Pilot. Ads searching for lost family. April 1, 1848.
Boston Pilot. Ads searching for lost family. August 12, 1848.
Boston Pilot. Ads searching for lost family. June 5, 1852.
Byron, Reginald. *Irish America.* Oxford University Press, 1999.
Dolan, Jay P. *The Irish Americans.* Bloomsbury Press, 2008.
Duncan, Stuart, William J. Aplington, Francis H. Dolan, Elizabeth Cummings, and Patricia Connolly. *LaSalle, Illinois: An Historical Sketch.* La Salle Centennial Committee, 1952.
Kenny, Kevin. *The American Irish.* Longman, Pearson Education, 2000.
Lee, J. J., and Marion R. Casey, eds. *Making the Irish American.* New York University Press, 2006.
Mitchell, Brian C. *The Paddy Camps: The Irish of Lowell, 1821–61.* University of Illinois Press, 1988.
Potter, George. *To the Golden Door.* Little, Brown, 1960.

New Hampshire

Babson, Deborah. *The History of St. Bernard's Parish 1852–2000.* Private printing, 2000.
Byrne, William. *History of the Catholic Church in the New England States.* Hurd & Everts, 1899.
Cheshire County History. "Map 5 1816 Cheshire County." Accessed March 8, 2026. https://www.vhist.com/nhcheshirecounty/the-early-maps/map-5-1816-cheshire-county/.
Garvin, Donna-Belle, and James L. Garvin. *On the Road North of Boston: NH Taverns and Turnpikes, 1700–1900.* New Hampshire Historical Society, 1988.

Griffin, S. G. *A History of the Town of Keene from 1732, When the Township Was Granted by Massachusetts, to 1874, When It Became a City.* Sentinel Printing, 1904.

Keene History Committee. *Upper Ashuelot: A History of Keene, New Hampshire.* City of Keene, New Hampshire, 1968.

Kingsbury, Frank B. *History of the Town of Surry, Cheshire County, New Hampshire: From Date of Severance from Gilsum and Westmoreland, 1769–1922.* Surry, New Hampshire, 1925.

Ladies Charitable Society. Historical papers. Historical Society of Cheshire County, 1815–1992.

New Hampshire Department of Transportation. Route 12 relocation. Right of way and as-built plans. Westmoreland-Surry-Keene. Project P2016 Federal Project F-162(2); F-190(2); F-222(8). 1948. https://maps.dot.nh.gov/reports/plan-inventory/.

Peery, Susan. *A Legacy of Good Works Since 1815: The History of the Ladies' Charitable Society of Keene, New Hampshire.* Historical Society of Cheshire County, c. 2003.

Rand, Thomas C. *A Sketch of Keene, the Gem of the Ashuelot Valley.* Keene, c. 1895.

Rumrill, Alan F. "A Moment in Local History: The 'Widest Paved Main Street in the World." *Keene Sentinel*, May 9, 2020.

Watson, Duncan. *Everyone's Trash: One Man Against 1.6 Billion Pounds.* Peter E. Randall, 2024.

Watson, Duncan. Interview with the author. February 2, 2024.

Westmoreland History Committee. *History of Westmoreland (Great Meadow) New Hampshire: 1741–1970, and Genealogical Data.* Westmoreland History Committee, 1976.

Wilber, Clifford C. *The Story of Central Square, Keene, New Hampshire.* 1945.

Wood, Frederic James. *The Turnpikes of New England and Evolution of the Same Through England, Virginia, and Maryland.* Marshall Jones, 1919.

Labor and Railroad History

Berger, John. *Pig Earth.* Vintage International Edition, 1979.

Berger, John. *Selected Essays.* Edited by Geoff Dyer. Pantheon Books, 2001.

Billings, Mathieu W. "Potent Legacies: The Transformation of Irish American Politics, 1815–1840." PhD diss., Department of History, Northern Illinois University, 2016.

Blue Ridge Railroad: *Daily Richmond Times*, February 1, 1850.

Buffalo and State Line Railroad: *Buffalo Commercial*, November 13, 1851.

C&O Riots: *Hartford Courant*, February 3, 1834; *Litchfield Enquirer*, February 6, 1834; *Martinsburg Gazette*, February 6, 1834; *Vermont Gazette*, February 11, 1834.

C&O "Treaty of Peace": *Alexandria Gazette*, February 4, 1834; *Maryland Gazette*, February 6, 1834; *Pittsburgh Gazette*, February 6, 1834; *York Gazette*, February 11, 1834.

Central Railroad: *Gallipolis Journal*, September 26, 1850; *Pittsburgh Daily Post*, September 2, 1850.

Croton Waterworks: *Adams Sentinel*, June 21, 1841; *Vicksburg Tri-Weekly Sentinel*, May 17, 1838.

Drinker, Henry S. *Tunneling, Explosive Compounds, and Rock Drills.* John Wiley & Sons, 1878.

Erie Railroad: *New York Herald*, February 16, 1857; *New York Times*, March 16, 1857.

Feldberg, Michael. *The Turbulent Era: Riot and Disorder in Jacksonian America*. Oxford University Press, 1980.

Great Western Railroad: *British Whig and General Advertiser for Canada West*, January 19, 1848; *Evening Post*, July 22, 1848; *Northern Tribune*, February 28, 1848.

Horner, Dan. "Solemn Processions and Terrifying Violence: Spectacle, Authority, and Citizenship During the Lachine Canal Strike of 1843." *Urban History Review* (Spring 2010).

Hudson Valley Railroad: *Public Ledger*, June 6, 1839; *Vermont Union Whig*, August 10, 1839.

Illinois and Michigan Canal: *Bloomington Observer*, January 13, 1838; *Native American*, December 1, 1838; *Native American*, January 26, 1839.

Kasson, John F. *Civilizing the Machine: Technology and Republican Values in America, 1776–1900.* Penguin Books, 1976.

Lachine Canal: *Buffalo Courier*, March 13, 1843; *Buffalo Courier*, March 20, 1843; *Buffalo Daily Gazette*, March 1, 1843; *Daily Eastern Argus*, March 1, 1843; *Democrat and Sentinel*, March 17, 1843; *New York Tribune*, September 8, 1842; *Ohio Democrat*, July 28, 1842; *Times Picayune*, March 2, 1843.

Lockport Free Press. "'Drunken, Dirty' Irish Build Canal." June 15, 1978.

Madison Railroad: *Pittsburgh Gazette*, September 16, 1837.

Mason, Matthew E. "'The Hands Here Are Disposed to Be Turbulent': Unrest Among the Irish Trackman of the Baltimore and Ohio Railroad, 1829–1851." *Labor History* 39, no. 3 (1999).

McMahon, Eileen M. "Canal Diggers, Church Builders: Dispelling Stereotypes of the Irish on the Illinois & Michigan Canal Corridor." *Journal of the Illinois State Historical Society* (Winter 2018).

Morris, Richard B. "Andrew Jackson, Strikebreaker." *American Historical Review* (October 1949).

New York and Erie Railroad: *Star of Freedom* (Leeds, England), March 27, 1847.

O'Brien, Andrew Leary. *The Journal of Andrew Leary O'Brien*. University of Georgia Press, 1946.

Perry, Jay Martin. "The Irish Wars Laborer Feuds on Indiana's Canals and Railroads in the 1830s." *Indiana Magazine of History*, September 2013.

Perry, Jay Martin. "Shillelaghs, Shovels, and Secrets: Irish Immigrant Secret Societies and the Building of Indiana Internal Improvements, 1835–1837." Master's thesis, University Graduate School, Department of History, Indiana University, December 2009.

Prince, Carl E. "The Great 'Riot Year': Jacksonian Democracy and Patterns of Violence in 1834." *Journal of the Early Republic* (Spring 1985).

Riots Around the Country: *New Hampshire Sentinel*, July 21, 1841; *New Hampshire Sentinel*, January 11, 1849; *New Hampshire Sentinel*, September 13, 1849.

Rorabaugh, W. J. *The Alcoholic Republic: An American Tradition*. Oxford University Press, 1979.

Schexnayder, Cliff. *Builders of the Hoosac Tunnel*. Peter E. Randall, 2015.

Steubenville and Indiana Railroad: *Albany Evening Journal*, February 17, 1852; *Buffalo Courier*, February 17, 1852; *Carroll Free Press*, February 20, 1852; *Irish American*, February 21, 1852; *Lancaster Gazette*, January 22, 1852; *Louisville Daily Courier*, February 12, 1852; *New Orleans Crescent*, February 4, 1852; *Pittsburgh Daily Post*, January 1, 1852; *Pittsburgh Daily Post*, February 1, 1852; *Portage Sentinel*, February 16, 1852; *Weekly Commercial*, March 5, 1852.

Utica Railroad: *Buffalo Weekly Republic*, March 5, 1850.

Wabash and Erie Canal: *Fayetteville Weekly Observer*, September 8, 1835; *Pittsburgh Gazette*, August 3, 1835; *Pittsburgh Gazette*, August 14, 1835; *Pittsburgh Gazette*, August 31, 1835.

Washington Railroad: *Alexandria Gazette*, June 23, 1834; *Maryland Gazette*, June 19, 1834; *National Gazette*, June 30, 1834.

Way, Peter. *Common Labor: Workers and the Digging of North American Canals, 1780–1860*. Johns Hopkins University Press, 1997.

Way, Peter. "Evil Humors and Ardent Spirits: The Rough Culture of Canal Construction Laborers." *Journal of American History* (March 1993).

Way, Peter. "Shovel and Shamrock: Irish Workers and Labor Violence in the Digging of the Chesapeake and Ohio Canal." *Labor History*, September 1989.

Welland Canal: *Boston Post*, September 7, 1842; *Lorain Republican*, September 28, 1842; *Pittsfield Sun*, September 22, 1842; *Sunbury Gazette*, October 1, 1842; *Tennessean*, September 19, 1842.

Cheshire Railroad

American Railroad Journal. "Cheshire Railroad." June 2, 1849.

American Railroad Journal. "Cheshire (N.H.) Railroad Opening." June 17, 1848.

Annual Report of the Directors of the Cheshire Railroad Company to the Corporation. J & J. W. Prentiss, 1846–1861. https://babel.hathitrust.org/cgi/pt?id=mdp.39015069987876&seq=1.

Blodget, Bradford G., and Richard R. Richards Jr. *Iron Roads of the Monadnock Region*. Vols. 1–2. Bauhan, 2019.

Historic American Engineering Record/New Hampshire Historic Property Documentation. *Cheshire Railroad Stone Arch Bridge*. 1847. https://www.historicdoc.com/reports/HAER-CheshireRRStone Arch.pdf.

Karr, Ronald Dale. *The Rail Lines of Southern New England.* Branch Line Press, 2017.

Licht, Walter. *Working for the Railroad*. Princeton University Press, 1983.

New Hampshire Sentinel. "Auction! Great Sale of Railroad Property!" October 19, 1848.

New Hampshire Sentinel. "Cheshire Railroad." February 24, 1847.

New Hampshire Sentinel. Death Notices. January 14, 1846.

New Hampshire Sentinel. Death Notices. June 17, 1847.

Report of the Railroad Commissioners of the State of New Hampshire, 1849.

Report of the Railroad Commissioners of the State of New Hampshire, 1850.

"Stone Arch Bridge." National Register of Historic Places Registration Form. 2012.

Vermont Chronicle. "Cheshire Railroad." March 17, 1847.

Vermont Phoenix. "Convention at Keene." January 5, 1844.

Vermont Union Whig. "Opening of the Cheshire Railroad to Keene N.H." May 25, 1848.

Wallace, R. Stuart, and Lisa Mausolf. *New Hampshire Railroad: Historic Context Statement*. Prepared for the New Hampshire Department of Transportation, April 2001.

Whiton, James M. *Railroads and Their Management*. Steam Printing Works of McFarland and Jenks, 1856.

Cheshire Railroad Riots

Cheshire Court of Common Pleas. State v. Murphy et al. Judgment Book, pp. 285–86, NhAr Box 52542. New Hampshire State Archives, September 1848.

Cheshire Republican and Farmer. "Court of Common Pleas, at Keene." September 21, 1848.

Cheshire Republican and Farmer. "The Trial of the Rioters." August 31, 1848.
New Hampshire Sentinel. "Rum and Riot." June 17, 1847.
New Hampshire Sentinel. "Serious Affray." August 24, 1848.
Vermont Phoenix. "Riot." June 24, 1847.

1848 Riot

Baltimore Sun. August 28, 1848.
Boston Evening Transcript. August 5, 1848.
Boston Evening Transcript. August 24, 1848.
Boston Pilot. September 9, 1848.
Buffalo Morning Express. August 29, 1848.
Daily Evening Transcript. August 24, 1848.
Louisville Daily Courier. September 2, 1848.
Morning Chronicle [London]. September 16, 1848.
New Orleans Crescent. September 5, 1848.
New York Daily Herald. August 26, 1848.
Vermont Chronicle. September 6, 1848.
Vermont Patriot and State Gazette. September 12, 1848.
Vermont Phoenix. September 1, 1848.
Vermont Watchman and State Journal. August 31, 1848.

Homecoming Denied

Air Force Historical Research Agency. Mission Planning, Reports and Analysis, Group/0379/Bombardment (Heavy), Squadron/0525/Bombardment (Heavy). 1943–1944.
Boston Globe. "Douglas Sloane 3d, Built Cathedral of Pines." December 22, 1972.
Cathedral of the Pines Book of Stories. N.d.
Hass, Robert. *The Short Course: "Reading Milosz."* Community of Writers, Olympic Valley, CA, January 20–February 24, 2022.
Mansfield, Howard. "A Family History of Water." In *Turn & Jump: How Time and Place Fell Apart*. Down East, 2010.
Mansfield, Howard. "Pages from an Ice Storm Journal." In *Dwelling In Possibility: Searching for the Soul of Shelter.* Bauhan, 2013.

McLellan, Peggy. Letter, December 15, 1993. Cathedral of the Pines Museum collection.

Missing Air Crew Report. 379th Bomb Group. February 25, 1944.

Peterborough Transcript. "Cites Aims, Ideals of Rindge Shrine: Sloane Tells Rotary of Growth of Cathedral of the Pines." June 1, 1950.

Peterborough Transcript. "Commemorate 1st. Anniv. at Rindge War Shrine." September 11, 1947.

Peterborough Transcript. "Pres. Compton of M.I.T. Buys Jaffrey Summer Home: Three Prominent Bay State Persons Secure Properties in Jaffrey and Rindge." March 24, 1938.

Peterborough Transcript. "Public Park Needed." May 18, 1950.

Peterborough Transcript. "Hold Double Funeral." Rindge News. February 3, 1949.

Peterborough Transcript. "Interlaken Sold." Rindge News. November 11, 1937.

Peterborough Transcript. "Last Letter Home." Rindge News. March 23, 1944.

Peterborough Transcript. "Missing in Action." Rindge News. March 6, 1944.

Peterborough Transcript. "Sloane-Allen." Weddings. November 19, 1942.

Peterborough Transcript. "State Opens New Picnic Area at Former Jaffrey CCC Camp." July 6, 1950.

Sloane, Douglas. "The Cathedral of the Pines and How It All Began." N.d.

Upton, Don. Interviews with the author, June 14, 2024, April 30, 2025.

Whitehouse, Arch. "Cathedral of the Pines." *Reader's Digest*, April 1947.

Falling from a Ferris Wheel

Daily News. "$2 Million Death Suit to Start Tomorrow." January 11, 1965.

Fortunato, Claudia. "Historic HHH: Fairyland Amusement Park." Patch: Half Hollow Hills, NY. June 22, 2011. http://halfhollowhills.patch.com/articles/historic-hhh-fairyland-amusement-park.

James, Henry. *English Hours.* Houghton Mifflin, 1905.

Lawrence, Josephine. *The Berry Patch.* Cupples & Leon, 1925.

Long Islander. "Baby, 2, Thrown Out of Ferris Wheel Car, Dies; Parents Hurt." July 2, 1964.
Long Islander. "Elwood's Hospital Is Closed." February 18, 1965.
Long Islander. "Fatal Accident Still Studied." July 9, 1964.
Long Islander. "Jury to Get Play Park Death Case." August 6, 1964.
Long Islander. "Operator of Park Escapes Jury Charge." September 17, 1964.
Mansfield, Howard. *I Will Tell No War Stories: What Our Fathers Left Unsaid About World War II*. Lyons Press, 2024.
Mansfield, Howard. "Veteran's Memorial Island—Peace by the Quarter Acre." In *Chasing Eden: A Book of Seekers*. Bauhan, 2021.
Mansfield, Howard. "Waiting (to Go Home)." In *At the End of Life: True Stories About How We Die*, edited by Lee Gutkind. Creative Nonfiction Books, 2011.
McCray, Charles. "Fortune Telling and American Religious Freedom." *Religion and American Culture: A Journal of Interpretation* 28, no. 2 (Summer 2018).
Munder, Fred. *Shaw v. Fairyland at Harvey's*. Supreme Court, New York State, February 11,1965.
New York Times. "Girl, 2, Dies After Fall from L.I. Ferris Wheel." June 30, 1964.
Shaw v. Fairyland at Harvey's Inc. Appellate Division of the Supreme Court, New York State, Second Department, June 20, 1966.
Springsteen, Bruce. "Secret Garden." Columbia Records, 1995.

The Clock of Now-Now-Now

Adams, Henry. *The Degradation of the Democratic Dogma*. Macmillan, 1919.
Alvarado, David, and Jason Sussberg, dirs. *We Are As Gods*. 94 min. Stripe Press, 2021.
Brand, Stewart. *Clock of the Long Now: Time and Responsibility*. Basic Books, 2008.
Camp, Susanna. "Portal to the Future: Alexander Rose and the 10,000-Year Clock." SmartUp. June 12, 2016. http://smartup.life/portal-to-the-future-alexander-rose-and-the-10000-year-clock.

Eno, Brian. "The Big Here and Long Now." Long Now Foundation. May 1, 2000. https://longnow.org/ideas/the-big-here-and-long-now/.

Hillis, Danny. "Danny Hillis Answers Frequently Asked Questions About the 10,000-Year Clock." Long Now Foundation. February 2024. https://longnow.org/clock/faq/.

Hillis, Danny. "The Millennium Clock." *Wired*, December 1995.

Karpf, David. "The 10,000-Year Clock Is a Waste of Time." *Wired*, January 2020.

Kelly, Kevin. "The Case for Optimism." Warp News. August 2, 2021. https://www.warpnews.org/premium-content/kevin-kelly-the-case-for-optimism/.

Kelly, Kevin. "Clock in the Mountain." Long Now Foundation. June 15, 2011. https://longnow.org/ideas/clock-in-the-mountain/.

Mansfield, Howard. *Turn & Jump: How Time & Place Fell Apart*. Down East, 2010.

Tweney, Dylan. "How to Make a Clock Run for 10,000 Years." *Wired*, June 2011.

Moment-Moment-Moment

Mansfield, Howard. "We Are Still in Eden—Awe on the American Plan." In *Chasing Eden: A Book of Seekers*. Bauhan, 2021.

Porte, Joel, ed. *Ralph Waldo Emerson: Essays and Lectures*. Library of America, 1983.

Tarrant, John. "2021 Spring Sesshin: A Donkey Sees a Well, a Well Sees a Donkey." Pacific Zen Institute. January 23, 2023. https://www.pacificzen.org/library/a-donkey-sees-a-well-a-well-sees-a-donkey/

Coda: The Fingerprints in the Brick

Price, Mark. "Historians Find Fingerprints of Long-Forgotten SC Slaves in 200-Year-Old Bricks." *Charlotte Observer*, July 3, 2024.

ABOUT THE AUTHOR

HOWARD MANSFIELD HAS WRITTEN A DOZEN BOOKS, INCLUDING *THE Bones of the Earth*; *The Same Ax, Twice*; *Chasing Eden*; *Dwelling in Possibility: Searching for the Soul of Shelter*; and *In the Memory House*, which *The New York Times* called a "wise and beautiful book." In his previous book *I Will Tell No War Stories: What Our Fathers Left Unsaid About World War II*, he "breaks through the wall of silence some war veterans maintain," said *Booklist*. "The result is an impeccably researched and beautifully written . . . history of all that is left unsaid in the aftermath of war and how that affects the next generation."

In his writing, Mansfield sifts through the commonplace and the forgotten to discover stories that tell us about ourselves and our place in the world. The critic Guy Davenport said, "Howard Mansfield has never written an uninteresting or dull sentence. All of his books are emotionally and intellectually nourishing. He is something like a cultural psychologist along with being a first-class cultural historian. He is humane, witty, bright-minded, and rigorously intelligent."

His essays and articles on history and architecture have appeared in such newspapers as *The New York Times*, *The Washington Post*, *The Christian Science Monitor*, *The Boston Globe*, and the *Los Angeles Times*, as well as in magazines, including *American Heritage*, *Metropolis*, *International Design*, *Yankee*, *Historic Preservation*, *Threepenny Review*, *Doubletake*, and *Creative Nonfiction*.

Mansfield's work has been honored with a gold medal for commentary for City and Regional Magazines, a silver medal from the Independent Publisher Book Awards, and he was a feature story finalist in the National City and Regional Magazine Awards. He received the 2026

Sarah Josepha Hale Award and an honorary doctor of humane letters from Franklin Pierce University.

He lives in Hancock, New Hampshire, with his wife, the writer Sy Montgomery.